THREE DAYS AT AGRA

THREE DAYS AT AGRA

A GUIDE TO PLACES OF INTEREST INCLUDING FATEHPUR SIKRI WITH HISTORY

H. A. NEWELL

GYAN

Published by

GYAN

Gyan Publishing House
5, Ansari Road
Daryaganj, New Delhi-110002
Phone: 011-47034999, 9811692060
E-mail: books@gyanbooks.com

Distribution Network
gyanbooks.com
India, USA, Canada, UK, Australia

ISBN: 978-93-7225-391-7 (PB)

First Published, 1922

2nd Impression 2025

Printed at: Gyan Press, Delhi.

THREE DAYS AT AGRA

Author: H. A. NEWELL

THREE DAYS AT AGRA

A Guide to Places of Interest, including Fatehpur Sikri, with History and Map

BY

LIEUT.-COL. H. A. NEWELL

Indian Army

FIFTH EDITION

CONTENTS

INTRODUCTION

No matter how experienced a traveller he may be, the new arrival at a strange place invariably feels at a disadvantage. This is particularly the case if sight-seeing be his object. He does not know just where to begin, and is uncertain in what order to take the places of interest he has come so far to visit. Enquiries pursued on the spot do not always tend to facilitate matters. He is frequently annoyed by finding that he has to retrace his steps and so cover the same ground twice. This leads to a vexatious waste of energy, time and cash. Nor is this all he has to suffer. The usual result of much sight-seeing is a severe fit of mental indigestion. Even under the most favourable conditions it is difficult to assimilate a host of hastily acquired impressions, and quite impossible if any confusion of ideas prevails.

In the hope of lessening the difficulties of sight-seeing at Agra I have drawn up an itinerary of the principal objects of interest in the city and immediate neighbourhood. The story and description of each place is briefly told. I have also included a short account of Fatehpur Sikri, the deserted city of Akbar. How it came to be founded is a romance without parallel in history. Its decline affords yet another striking example of the triumph of the practical over the claims of sentiment.

To archæologists the abandoned capital offers one of the most absorbing fields of research in Hindustan. Its forsaken palaces, echoing courts and mighty gateways represent the perfection of Moghul architecture under Akbar. This famous style sprang into existence with the Great Moghul, reached its zenith during the reign of his grandson, Shah Jahan, and perished with Aurangzib, the last of the four really powerful Emperors to sway the sceptre of the Moghuls.

When bringing out a third edition of my little guide to Agra I ventured to enlarge, and, I hope, improve upon the two earlier issues. Experience had taught me that visitors to India are less superficially minded than I had been led to imagine. Contrary to general belief the majority are not satisfied with merely being told which of our wonderful buildings to look at, of glancing at them and then hurrying past. They want to understand what they see, to know something definite about those master minds which have left such outward and visible signs of their greatness behind as cause modern man to marvel, and to question whether the world is such a gainer by civilization as he professes it.

The last few years have witnessed a marked increase of public interest in historical matters. The same may be said of archæology, a subject once regarded as dry as dust by all but the erudite few, but which is rapidly extending its vivid appeal to popular imagination. Encouraged by these facts I am now venturing to trespass still further upon the rich Tom Tiddler's ground of history. The additional data contained in my fifth edition is chiefly gleaned from such authoritative sources as the personal memoirs of Baber, founder of the Moghul empire, the *Ain-i-Akbari*, and the *Storia do Mogor.* The last-named work is from the pen of Niccolao Manucci, a Venetian, who emigrated from Europe in 1653 in the suite of Henry Bard, Viscount Bellomont, the English Ambassador despatched by Charles II to the Courts of Persia and Delhi. Manucci landed at Surat in January 1656, proceeded to Agra and thence to Delhi. On the way thither Lord Bellomont died at Hodal, beyond Muttra, on June 26, 1656. Subsequently his remains were conveyed to Agra for burial. Manucci was then a youth of about seventeen. At Delhi he enlisted, as an artilleryman at Rs. 80 a month, in the service of the heir apparent, Prince Dara Shekch, the eldest and favourite son of Shah Jahan. Two years later Manucci was present at the fatal battle between Dara, and his two brothers, Aurangzib and Murad Baksh. Thereafter Manucci fled to Agra where the old Emperor Jahan was speedily made a prisoner in his own fort by Aurangzib. Manucci recounts these and many other historical events as an eyewitness. Hence their value.

In presuming to write of Agra, and attempt a description of its peerless monument, the Taj Mahal, I must acknowledge my indebtedness to Lord Curzon of Kedleston for kindly pointing out an error I committed in my first edition when speaking of the beautiful bronze lamp, inlaid with gold and silver, which he presented to this shrine. The lamp was made in Egypt. It swings above the cenotaph of the Empress in the chamber over the vault wherein the mortal remains of Shah Jahan, and of his beloved consort, await the trumpet call to which all must answer when sounds the reveille.

H. A. NEWELL, LIEUT.-COL.,

Indian Army.

AGRA

SINCE the days of Imperial Rome Europe has never again acknowledged one city as paramount. Not so with India. Throughout the ages one capital has arisen, then another, towards which all others in the great peninsula have turned in homage.

Various causes have led to the transfer of supremacy from one famous Indian city to another. Sometimes conquest was responsible for the change. At others the whim of a sovereign sufficed to transform a flourishing metropolis into a desert waste of bricks and mortar, raising in its stead an insignificant village to the proud position of capital of an empire.

During the reign of Akbar alone, Delhi, Agra, and Fatehpur Sikri were, in turn, the head-quarters of Moghul power.

No doubt the strategical advantages of Agra, its superior position upon the banks of the Jumna, and its proximity to the coveted kingdoms of the Deccan influenced Akbar to choose it as his capital in preference to Delhi, the old metropolis of Hindustan. The change was effected upon the Great Moghul's return from a punitive expedition against Malwa. His first care was to demolish the ancient earthen wall erected by the Pathan monarchs, and replace it with one of hewn stone quarried at Fatehpur Sikri.

Finding the town partly in ruins, and the palace of the Lodi Kings far from his liking, Akbar determined to reconstruct Agra on entirely new lines. To this end he planned a city in keeping with the splendour of his mighty empire.

The result of his efforts, and those of his successors, was to convert what had been a fortified town of secondary consideration, into the most beautiful, the wealthiest and most famous capital in India.

Prior to the coming of Akbar, and its subsequent metamorphosis into the head-quarters of the Moghul Empire, Agra owed its chief importance to its situation on the banks of the Jumna, then the highway for traffic between the rich delta of Bengal and the heart of India. Mention of the place is made by Ptolemy, in whose map it is spelt Agara. Another discrepancy is the latitude which differs considerably from that given in modern geographies.

From prehistoric times it appears to have been a fortified position, and to have constituted the frontier defence of the Aryans, who penetrated to the plain between the Ganges and Jumna. As such it was constantly attacked by their hereditary enemies settled in the highlands of Central India.

Early in the thirteenth century the Afghans, and other tribes from the north, began to people the neighbourhood and establish kingdoms, until, finally, their power extended from Agra to Delhi.

The last and best known of these Afghan dynasties was that of the Lodis. It was a monarch of this line, Sikandar Lodi, who promoted Agra to be his capital in 1500. A.D. His head-quarters are commonly reputed to have been at Sikandarah a village some five miles distant. However this may be, he spared no pains in strengthening the fort of Agra, a stronghold of very great antiquity, said to have stood on the site now covered by Akbar's citadel. Other authorities, however, place it on the opposite bank of the Jumna.

In 1526 Agra was occupied by Babar. On entering the citadel the victorious monarch solemnly announced that his invasion of India was no mere raid but a permanent conquest. With this the descendant of Taimur Shah—the terrible Tamerlane of European historians—assumed the style and title of Emperor of Hindustan. In his memoirs Baber describes the famous battle of Panipat, near Delhi, to which he owed his amazing rise to power. His little army of twelve thousand routed a vastly superior force a hundred thousand strong, supplemented by nearly a thousand elephants. For this achievement he bestows particular praise upon his bowmen and artillery. By his order the gun carriages had been coupled together, Turkish fashion, with thongs of twisted bull hide. When the sun had mounted 'a spear high' the conflict began. By midday he was master of Hindustan with naught between him and Delhi and Agra but distance. The corpse of Sultan Ibrahim was found on the stricken field surrounded by some five or six thousand slain. Instantly the head of the defeated monarch was struck off and conveyed to Baber at the hour of evening prayers. Forthwith the victor offered up thanks to the God of Battles, and despatched his son, Humayun, to occupy Agra and seize the treasury. Upon arrival the prince was greeted by the widow of the Gwalior Rajah, who had fallen at Panipat. Together with other members of the family she presented him with a peace offering of splendid jewels. To quote Baber on the subject: 'Among these was one famous diamond the Koh-i-nur (Mountain of Light) which had been acquired by Ala-ud-Din. It is so valuable that a judge of diamonds estimated it at half the daily expense of the whole world. On my arrival Humayun offered it to me, but I gave it back to him as a present.'

Baber proved a magnanimous conqueror. He settled the revenues of a district upon Ibrahim's mother, and assigned her a palace to live in about a mile below Agra. The old Begam, however, was not to be propitiated. On learning that the conqueror had employed four Hindu cooks, formerly in the service of her son, she sent for the taster, Ahmad, and authorized him to bribe one of these cooks with the promise of four districts, as reward for poisoning Baber. Thereafter she despatched two female slaves with an ounce of poison. Baber was seized with vomiting after partaking of hare, a dish to which he was especially partial. His suspicions being aroused he commanded the remainder to be given to a dog. The animal ate it and died. This led to the discovery of the plot. Baber condemned the taster to be flayed alive, and the cook hacked in pieces. One female slave was trampled to death by elephants, and the other shot with a matchlock. The old Begam was placed under arrest. In his memoirs Baber merely hints at her fate in the sentence: 'She, too, pursued by her guilt will one day meet with due retribution.'

Baber describes his arrival at Agra. Upon reaching the suburbs of the city he halted for the night at the Palace of Sulaiman. 'As this position was very far from the fort I moved on next morning and took up my quarters in the Palace of Jilal Khan.' Contrary to expectation he found that the citadel had not surrendered to Humayun. The prince had contented himself with barring all egress therefrom. Baber continues: 'On Thursday, the 28th of Rejab, about the hour of afternoon prayers, I entered Agra and took up my abode in Sultan Ibrahim's palace. . . . The Saturday following I began to examine and to distribute the treasure. I gave Humayun 700,000*l* and over and above this a palace, of which no account, or inventory had been taken. To some Amirs I gave 100,000*l* to others 80,000*l*, 70,000*l* and 60,000*l*. On the Afghans, Hazaras, Arabs, Baluchis and others in the army I bestowed suitable gratuities according to rank. Merchants, men of letters, in a word every person with me carried off presents. To each man and woman, slave or free, in the country of Kabul, I sent one rupee as a gift.'

From this it would appear that the Agra treasury yielded a prize of war worthy the name. In spite of this rich harvest the army grew increasingly restless and homesick. Even the Generals urged a speedy retirement to Kabul. The celebrated Khwajah Khan went to such lengths as to scribble a couplet on the walls of his house :—

> Should I succeed in recrossing Sind,
> Plague take me if ever I wish for Hind.

Nor was their discontent without foundation. Baber himself records : 'When I came to Agra it was the hot season. All the inhabitants had fled from terror so that we could not procure grain, nor provender either for ourselves, or our horses. Out of hostility and hatred to us the villagers had taken to rebellion and thieving. The roads became impassable.' In spite of the scarcity he gave 'a great feast in the grand hall, which is adorned with the peristyle of stone pillars under the dome, in the centre of Sultan Ibrahim's private palace.'

His early impressions are particularly interesting : vide, 'It always appears to me that one of the chief defects of Hindustan is the want of artificial water courses. I had intended, wherever I might fix my residence, to construct water wheels, to produce an artificial stream, and to lay out a regularly planned pleasure ground. Shortly after coming to Agra I passed the Jumna with this object in view and examined the country to pitch upon a fit spot. The whole was so ugly and detestable that I recrossed the river repulsed and disgusted.' Finding no better site, however, he set to work to lay out the desired pleasance. Furthermore he constructed a road from Agra to Kabul. Masonry pillars, twenty-four feet high, were erected at every stage of fourteen miles. Post houses were also established all along the Badshah-ka rasta, or King's Highway, at regular intervals of sixteen miles. Each had a supply of six horses and accommodation for courier and grooms.

Baber's rule at Agra lasted four years. He died in that city on December 26, 1530, aged forty-eight. His remains lay in state in Ram Bagh, the garden residence which he had constructed overhanging the Jumna. From thence they were transported to Kabul for burial. There, by his wish, they rest on the hillside in the pleasance whereof he wrote: 'When the argwhan flowers are in bloom, the yellow mingling with the red, I know of no place in the world to compare with it.' His son, Humayun, made his head-quarters at Delhi, where he met his death by falling down a flight of stone steps in the old fort. His tomb ranks amid the architectural glories of the imperial city.

When Akbar decided to transfer his capital to Agra, and entirely rebuild the metropolis of the Lodi kings, he summoned workmen from far and near to help in the task. North, south, east and west, contributed skilled artisans, clever architects, cunning sculptors, artists and craftsmen, versed in every branch of external ornament and interior decoration.

The citadel was begun in 1565, and took over eight years to build. More than a thousand masons were constantly employed upon it, and the total cost amounted to Rs. 3,000,000.

Designed in the form of a crescent, Akbar's great red castle on the banks of the Jumna is the largest ever erected in India. The sandstone, used in the construction, was quarried at Fatehpur Sikri. Thanks to its extraordinary durability the fort is in a perfect state of preservation, and might, so far as any sign of decay is apparent, have been built within the last couple of decades rather than over three centuries ago.

Desirous of pleasing their sovereign the rajas and wealthy omrahs vied with one another in their efforts to embellish the capital. Luxurious mansions sprang up along the banks of the Jumna. Beautiful gardens were laid out with water-channels, fountains and lakes, and planted with shady trees flowers and fruit.

Akbar was particularly fond of fruit, his favourite varieties being the melon, pomegranate and grape.

Contemporary writers speak of Akbar's cities as very beautiful by reason of the splendour of the palaces, terraces, gateways and towers, the trains of gaily caparisoned elephants, and glittering cavalcades of princes and nobles. The streets however, were narrow, crowded and far from clean, and the poorer residences lacked windows. The houses of the rich were very fine, being surrounded by lovely gardens. They formed a sharp contrast to the dwellings of the masses—squalid huts of mud and straw.

The Ain-i-Akbari, or Institutes of Akbar, compiled at that Emperor's command by the celebrated historian Abul Fazl, contains the following account:—

'Agra is a large city, the air of which is esteemed very healthy. The river Jumna runs through it for five Cose. On both banks are delightful houses and gardens inhabited by people of all nations, and where are displayed the productions of every climate. His Majesty has erected a fort of red stone, the like of which no traveller has ever beheld. It contains alone five hundred stone buildings of surprising construction, in the Bengal, Gujarat and other styles. The artificers have decorated them with beautiful paintings. At the eastern gate are carved in stone two elephants, with their riders, of exquisite workmanship. In former times Agra was a village dependent upon Byaneh, where Sikander Lodi kept his court. Here His Majesty has founded a most magnificent city. On the opposite side of the river is the Charbagh (Four Gardens) a monument of the magnificence of that inhabitant of Paradise, Humayun. The author of this book was born on that side of the river. There are the tombs of his ancestors together with that of his elder brother Sheikh Faizi (The Poet Laureate). Sheikh Ala-ud-Mujzoob, Mir Ruffi-ud-Din Sufi and many other eminent personages are also interred there.'

After the Great Moghul had been laid to rest outside the city walls in the Garden of Bihishtabad at Sikundarah, his son Jahangir added still further to the magnificence of Agra by building a tomb to his father, and another to his father-in-law, Itmad-ud-Daulah. It remained for Jahan, however, to render Agra peerless among cities by reason of the Taj Mahal, that wonderful 'Crown of Palaces,' wherein he and his Empress lie buried.

During his reign, Manucci the Venetian, known to posterity as author of the *Storia do Mogor*, arrived at Agra in the suite of Viscount Bellomont. It was the hot weather of 1656. Manucci describes how the Governor of the city assigned the English Ambassador a handsome house to stay in. There he was waited upon by some of his fellow countrymen employed in the English factory. 'After several visits they invited him to their house, where they gave him a splendid feast, with dressed meats and beverages after their style.' In a few days, Lord Bellomont started for Delhi, which city Jahan had made his capital. Beyond Muttra, at a place called Hodal, the envoy of Charles II was seized with violent pains and died. His remains were brought back to Agra for burial. Of this city Manucci says: 'Akbar decided to leave Fathabad (Fatehpur Sikri) and found another city twelve leagues off on the bank of the Jumna. For this purpose he chose the village of Agra in the year 1563. It was named Akbarabad, that is to say built by Akbar. He gave an order that his palaces should be made of copper. But it was represented to him that this could not be done. Enough metal could not be procured to erect lofty palaces such as the king desired. Another reason was that they would not be habitable in the hot season, on account of the high temperature, nor in the winter, from the great cold. Thus he abandoned this project and constructed his palaces and the fortress of red-hewn stones of great size.

The city has a great open plain on the bank of the River Jumna, which, as it were, divides it in half on the eastern side. The town is a large one, with a circumference of twelve leagues, and is surrounded by many gardens. It is not walled, but has, nevertheless, great gateways in the principal streets. The fortress is placed on the bank of the river, and has a ditch which can be filled with water therefrom. On both sides the fortress is adorned with beautiful palaces. On the other side of the river, is a large garden, a village and many tombs.

During the time that the said city was being brought to perfection the king's amusement was to mount on a mad elephant, simply to make it combat with another.'

Manucci dilates upon the constant rebellions against which Akbar had to contend in the immediate neighbourhood, as well as in more distant parts of his dominions. These the Venetian attributes to discontent caused by taxation. He says: 'Akbar had a great deal of trouble with these rebels. After returning home victorious he was forced to send his captains against them several times. . . . Every time that a General won a victory the heads of the villagers were sent as booty to the city of Agra, to be displayed in the royal square before all the people, as a proof of their success. After twenty-four hours the heads were removed to the imperial highway. Here they were hung from the trees, or deposited in holes on pillars built for this purpose. Each pillar could accommodate one hundred heads. Once I saw ten thousand of them, shaven and with huge moustaches, mostly reddish in colour. In the thirty four years that I dwelt in this Moghul kingdom I travelled often from Agra to Delhi. Every time there was a number of fresh heads on the road-side, and many bodies hanging from the trees, punished thus for highway robbery. Passers-by are obliged to hold their noses on account of the odour of the dead, and hasten their steps out of apprehension of the living.'

From the hour of Jahan's death in the Saman Burj, or Jasmine Tower, a prisoner in his splendid palace, Agra's greatness began to wane. Delhi was the capital of Hindustan and the head-quarters of succeeding Emperors.

Abandoned by his descendants Akbar's metropolis would have dropped to the level of an ordinary provincial town but for its buildings. These rank amid the greatest achievements of Moghul architecture.

In modern times Agra was the capital of the United Provinces prior to 1857. After the mutiny the seat of Government was transferred to Allahabad. Now it gives its name to a district and division in the United Provinces.

Agra lies 841 miles from Calcutta and is an important railway centre, two main lines branching thence, southwards, to Bombay. The town is of some commercial importance, containing a number of mills, factories and numerous educational establishments.

Even in Akbar's time the name Agra was not confined to the city. It embraced the large and wealthy Subah, or province of Agra, once Biana. This was a compact division extending from Kalpi to Rewari, and from Aligarh to the southern boundary of Narwar. Besides the Moghul capital it included Gwalior and other walled towns and fortresses.

The land revenue exceeded a quarter of a million.

The name Akbarabad, which appears on coinage of the period, applied to the citadel, now known as Agra Fort.

ARTS AND CRAFTS

Baber had been much impressed by the amount of skilled labour ready to hand in India. In his memoirs he comments upon the fact: 'Another convenience of Hindustan is that workmen of every profession and trade are innumerable and without end. For any work or employment there is always a set available to whom the same employment and trade have descended from father to son for ages.'

Similarly the Ain-i-Akbari comments: 'In Agra they manufacture blankets and fine stuffs. Here, too, are assembled artificers of every denomination.'

As is to be expected in the city famed for such masterpieces of mosaic as the Taj Mahal, and the Durgah of Itmad-ud-Daulah, inlaying in stone is an industry for which Agra is still celebrated. The art is not indigenous, but was imported from Italy in the sixteenth century. When Akbar collected clever craftsmen from all quarters of his dominions, to construct and embellish his citadel, he set an example which his immediate successors followed prior to embarking upon any great architectural venture.

The first specimen of *pietra dura* appears on the tomb of Itmad-ud-Daulah, father-in-law to Jahangir Shah. It was the work of Italians. These found many apt imitators among the Indian masons. The result was that the art took root in Agra, where it has been handed down, from father to son, with the traditional fidelity of the East.

The mosaic is not that of modern Roman jewellers. It is the older form of *pietra dura* revived by the Florentines during the Renaissance. The process consists of cutting thin slices of variously coloured precious stones to the exact shape of petal, eaf or other ornament. These are cemented into white, or black marble with such exquisite precision that even a microscope fails to reveal any join in a rose composed of sixty fragments.

Carving is also practised at Agra. Models of the Taj are faithfully executed in white marble. Fatehpur Sikri produces miniature reproductions, in soapstone and red sandstone, of the celebrated Moghul ruins for which the deserted city is renowned. Finely chiselled inkstands, boxes, stone dishes and trays are also attractive souvenirs.

Cunningly fashioned clay fruit and vegetables are other specialities of Agra. They are so carefully moulded and coloured as to pass muster for real until taken in the hand.

Agra is renowned for its pure silken fabrics, its embroideries and its carpets.

Of this industry Abul Fazl comments: 'His Majesty (Akbar) has given such encouragement to this manufacture that the carpets of Persia and Tartary are thought no more of. Great numbers of carpet weavers are settled here, and derive immense profit from their labour. The best carpets are made at Agra, Fatehpur Sikri and Lahore. In the royal workshops a carpet measuring twenty yards seven terrujes, by six yards is made for Rs. 1,810, against a valuation of Rs. 2,750 set upon it by those skilled in the business.'

A sharp line of demarcation divides Indian carpets into two classes, those of purely Hindu origin, their designs dating from the most remote antiquity, and those introduced by the Saracens, who were indebted for the art to Persia.

To the former category belong cotton carpets, known as dharis and satrangis. The patterns are wonderfully effective while the colouring is a daring contrast of rich tints of a depth and tone never encountered west of Suez. Nothing in the designs betrays any taint of external influence. These have remained true to tradition through countless centuries and are archaic in their simplicity. Weavers of dharis and satrangis still repeat the vivid chocolate and blue stripes, the diamonds and squares, with now and again a touch of gold or silver, which their remote ancestors wove prior to the influx of the Aryans across the Indus, or Manu compiled his celebrated code.

If the patterns common to dharis and satrangis are purely Indian in conception, and date from prehistoric times, the same cannot be claimed for pile carpets. These are Indian in execution only. The industry dates from the sixteenth century when the Saracens first introduced it into Hindustan from Persia.

In their pile carpets, Indian weavers have mostly been content to copy their early masters; hence the majority of designs are Persian, while all reveal Iranian influence of some sort.

At first sight carpet-weaving seems invitingly easy, but first appearances are notoriously deceptive. It is so in this case. Known as kalin, or kalicha, the foundation of pile carpets is a warp of sturdy cotton, or hempen threads, strung vertically on to a wooden frame. Seated on the ground the weaver proceeds to twist short lengths of wool, or silk in and out of the strings, taking care that the two ends protrude in front. Each row is held in place by the woof, a line of wool running across the warp after the manner of darning. Every now and again the weaver pauses in his swift manipulation of colours to comb down his work with a short wooden kangi, or comb. Finally the whole is clipped all over to render the pile of uniform depth, and so ensure a smooth, velvety surface.

The lament is often heard that Indian carpets have sadly deteriorated in quality. Unfortunately this is only too true of many industries. The fault, however, does not lie with the workman. It rests at the door of modern commercial methods.

Exquisitely skilful with his hands though he is, the Indian craftsman is no mere manual labourer. He is an artist. This is true of the carpet weaver. His is the artistic temperament and he suffers from the defects of his qualities. He works better without a fixed plan. His inspiration must not be cramped as to design, time or too small a price. Leave him a margin and allow him fair play. Happy in the knowledge that he is appreciated, and that his family will not starve if he elaborates a design, he will turn out as fine a carpet as did his ancestors in the days before mere man was called upon to compete with machinery.

AKBAR, THE GREAT MOGHUL

The month was October and the year A.D. 1542. A pitiless sun beat down upon the arid desert of Scind. Its withering rays shone full upon a small band of horsemen, some seven or eight in number, intensifying their already acute sufferings, and those of the few camels trailing in a tired line behind. Speechless with thirst, hunger and fatigue, the only sound made by the little cävalcade was when a horseman raised his voice to urge on his exhausted mount. Presently one of the foremost animals sank down to die in the desert. Immediately the rider disentangled himself from the saddle and, approaching a young girl, demanded her horse. It was one which he had lent to her, and he now needed it for his own use. The desert does not tend to breed carpet knights.

The girl obeyed him and slipped down on to the hot sand. At this a second rider, evidently the leader of the expedition, approached. Dismounting, he lifted the weary girl on to his own horse. For a while he tramped along beside her, then fell back and climbed on to a baggage camel.

The actors in this pitiful little drama of the desert were no ordinary travellers. The tired girl was Hamida Banu Begam, better known by her imperial title Maryam Mahal, Our Lady of the Palace. At the time she was fifteen years of age. Humayun, the Emperor, had met her in Lahore, while on a visit to his brother Hindal's mother. With the Emperor it had been a case of love at first sight. So passionately enamoured did he become of the fair Persian that nothing would satisfy him but an immediate marriage.

Within a year of their wedding day, the defeated monarch of Hindustan and his girl bride were flying for their lives before the victorious army of Sher Shah, in a desperate effort to reach the court of Tahmasp, Shah of Persia.

The ungallant cavalier, to reclaim his horse and so force his Empress to dismount, was Roshan Beg, one of Humayun's officers, while it was Humayun himself who trudged footsore over the desert that his wife might ride.

The story is told by Jauhar, ewer bearer to Humayun, and the faithful companion of that monarch's many vicissitudes of fortune. The memoirs go on to relate how that evening the Fort of Umarkot was reached. There, under the kindly shade of a large tree, Akbar, the Great Moghul, was born to Hamida on October 15, A.D. 1542.

When the good news was brought to Humayun, the Emperor called for a pod of musk. Breaking it he distributed the contents among his followers saying: 'This is all the present I can make you on the birth of my son, whose fame, I trust, will one day be expanded all over the world, even as the perfume of this musk now fills this apartment!'

Humayun's exile lasted for thirteen years. During the first four, he stayed at the Court of Tahmasp, Shah of Persia, passing the remainder in Kabul, ruling over his father's old kingdom and original heritage. Meanwhile his supplanter,

Sher Shah, rose to greatness in Hindustan. It was not as a conqueror, however, but as a statesman, that Sher Shah excelled. The laws which he framed, the administrative reforms he inaugurated, his fiscal policy, his genius as a ruler, an organizer and unionist, coupled with the indefatigable industry with which he worked for the general good, sowed the seeds of that consolidated empire from which Akbar was to reap so splendid a harvest in years to come.

No doubt the golden day of India's greatness would have dawned earlier but for the death of Sher Shah on May 22, 1545. While directing the siege of Kalingar, the ablest monarch Hindustan ever knew, was killed by the explosion of a powder magazine, near to which he stood, and which was accidentally struck by a random shot from the enemies' batteries.

Friction among the successors of Sher Shah gave Humayun his opportunity. He marched against Lahore, and then Agra, with the result that the autumn of 1555 saw him once more installed as Emperor at Delhi. He did not live to enjoy his reconquered greatness. On the 26th of January, 1556, he expired in his capital at the age of forty-eight. His death was caused by a fall down the stone stairs of his library in the citadel.

Abul Fath Jalal-ad-Din Muhammed Akbar Padishah Ghazi was in his fourteenth year when he succeeded to the masnad. The news of his father's death reached him on February, 15. He was then at Kalanur, near Amritsar encamped with Bairam Khan, the celebrated Turkoman general who had been despatched to pacify the Panjab.

Akbar at once assumed the title of Emperor. Simultaneously Bairam Khan was appointed Prime Minister in addition to his post of Commander-in-Chief of the Army. His sterling qualities as a military leader, coupled with the fact that his wife was a sister of Humayun and therefore aunt to the boy king, made it evident that Bairam Khan was the fitting person to be guardian to the youthful sovereign.

Akbar was not destined to become master of Hindustan without striking a blow. His opponent was Hemu, the celebrated Hindu, who had raised himself from the position of corn-chandler to that of Commander-in-Chief to Adil Shah Sur, the Afghan usurper, whose overthrow of Sher Shah's son and successor, and the disputes resulting therefrom, had given Humayun his opportunity of reconquest.

No sooner had Humayun breathed his last than Hemu collected an army together in Bengal. Advancing swiftly, he seized Agra and Delhi after slight resistance, in fact he met with no determined opposition until he reached Panipat, the famous battlefield whereon the destinies of Hindustan had so often been determined. Here he was faced by the Moghul army under Bairam Khan. The fourteen-year old Akbar was also present.

The fortunes of the day were decided by an arrow that pierced Hemu through the forehead. Mortally wounded, the ill-starred leader was dragged from his howdah and brought before Bairam Khan. As the vanquished enemy lay senseless on the ground the Moghul general handed Akbar a sword wherewith to deliver the *coup de grace.* Even at that early age Akbar revealed traces of that generosity which was to be his dominant characteristic through life. The lad merely touched the prostrate foe on the neck, then burst into tears. Angered by this display of sensibility, Bairam warned him that mistaken clemency had often proved fatal to kings. So saying, he struck off Hemu's head. This he despatched to Kabul. The body was exposed on one of the gates of Delhi, a warning to rebels.

By the victory of Panipat, Akbar found himself master of Hindustan. The rival claimant, Adil Sher Sur, died shortly afterwards in Bengal, leaving the boy Emperor an unrestricted field wherein to work out his great destiny.

During the first five years of his long reign Akbar remained under the tutelage of Bairam Khan. He was also swayed by his nurse, Maham Anka, to whom he was much attached. The former was a good influence and worked for the welfare of the sovereign and of the realm. Unfortunately, that of the nurse was not an unmixed blessing. She is credited with having intrigued to advance her son, Adham Khan, at the expense of Bairam. Finally secret friction between the Emperor and his guardian broke into open host lity. The Commander-in-Chief took up arms against his sovereign, was defeated and brought a prisoner before him. Akbar was then nineteen years old. He pardoned his great general, but ordered him on a pilgrimage to Mecca. While on his way to the port of embarkation the man to whom the youthful Padishah owed his empire was ignominiously stabbed by a Pathan.

From then on Akbar ruled alone. The next fifteen years were chiefly passed at the head of his army in the field. Constant outbreaks in various parts of his dominions called for ceaseless activity in their suppression. Such short intervals of peace as he enjoyed were devoted to sport and to building.

In 1565 Akbar commenced his splendid citadel at Agra, preferring to make that city his capital rather than Delhi. Four years later, namely, in 1569, he began to build Fatehpur Sikri, or City of Victory, at Sikri, a village some twenty-four miles from Agra. This long continued his favourite residence, being doubly dear to him as the birthplace of his two sons.

From his succession until he was well advanced in the thirties, Akbar was perpetually engaged in conquest. The record of his achievements in this direction furnishes a surprising example of endurance, persevering activity and physical strength.

He was only fourteen when the decisive battle of Panipat was fought in November, 1556. This made him master of Delhi and Agra. In 1558 Gwalior was subdued. Jaunpur and Ramtambhor were reduced in 1559. Malwa capitulated in 1561, and Burhanpur in Kandish was stormed in 1562. After a desperate defence by Jai Mall the celebrated Rajput stronghold of Chitagarh was carried in 1567. This brought Rajputana temporarily under Moghul dominion. In 1572 Akbar entered Ahmadabad. After subduing Gujarat he carried his victorious standard into Surat, Cambay and Barodah. Bengal acknowledged his authority in 1577. Kashmir was annexed in 1587, Janagarh in 1591, and Kandahar in 1593. The wealthy kings of the Deccan were humbled and compelled to become feudatories. To commemorate this most auspicious victory an immense gateway, known as the Buland Darwaza, was erected at Fatehpur Sikri. That it was intended as a triumphal arch is proved by the inscription: 'His Majesty, the King of Kings, whose court is Paradise, the shadow of God, Jahal-ad-Din Muhammed Akbar Padishah, conquered the Deccan,' etc.

The Ain-i-Akbari states that the Great Moghul never assembled his entire army when undertaking an expedition. His reason was that the passage of so many people through a district would have reduced the countryside to famine. Nor was provisioning the sole difficulty. It would have been impossible to provide shelter for the troops not to speak of the swarms of followers. Akbar introduced his own method of encamping. Primarily a space, 1,530 yards long, was set apart for the Gulalbar, or royal enclosure. It was surrounded by wooden walls strengthened with straps of leather, and so constructed for transport purposes, as to fold up into a comparatively small compass. Entrance to it was through doors provided with locks and keys. At the eastern end stood a pavilion containing fifty-four rooms, each of which measured twenty-four yards by fourteen yards. The centre was occupied by the Chaubin Rowty, a frame building consisting of ten pillars, wooden cross beams, and roof and walls of woven reeds. Adjoining this were a number of pavilions. Near by rose a two-storeyed edifice where the Emperor attended divine worship. From the upper floor he looked down upon the nobility and others, who assembled daily to pay their respects at sunrise. Beyond again were twenty-four Chaubin Rowties, ten yards long by six wide. These were reserved for favourites of the imperial harem. Further on was a great tent, sixty yards square, composed of carpets. It was the guard-house occupied by female sentries posted in the first enclosure of the seraglio.

In front stretched a plain 150 yards long and 100 yards broad flanked by magnificent tents. Down the entire length every sixth foot of ground was marked by an eighteen foot pole topped by a glittering brass ornament. Before each of these a sentinel was posted. The middle of the maidan was sacred to the Numgirah, an awning supported by four poles. Here Akbar sat every evening conversing with a privileged few. In addition to the structures mentioned, there were innumerable others for the Begams, the princes and great ministers of State. Little wonder that the transport of the royal enclosure called for the services of a hundred elephants, five hundred camels, four hundred carts and a hundred men. These travelled with an escort of five hundred cavalry, and a personnel which included five hundred pioneers, a hundred watercarriers, fifty carpenters, fifty tentmakers, fifty linkmen, thirty leatherworkers, a hundred and fifty sweepers and a thousand other menials.

While busily engaged in building up his empire by repeated conquest, Akbar was equally actively employed in consolidating what he had won. By every means in his power he sought the welfare of all subject to him. Realizing that union makes strength he brought his powers to bear on solving the problem of how best to adapt one supreme rule to the needs, prejudices, aspirations and conditions of directly opposing races, naturally hostile to one another for reasons of nationality and religion.

The task he had set himself was no light one. Fortunately he was gifted with a peculiarly receptive and open mind and wide sympathies. Added to these qualities he was an eager student of history, appreciating that its pages contain the most profitable lessons a ruler can learn. 'Daily some capable person reads to His Majesty, who hears every book from beginning to end. He always marks the place where he leaves off with the day of the month. The reader is paid according to the number of pages. There is hardly a work of science, of genius or of history but has been read to His Majesty, He is not tired by repetition but always listens with great avidity.' Akbar was wise enough and humble enough to recognize that his predecessor, Sher Shah, had grasped the difficulties of just such another situation as the one he found himself called upon to face. Accordingly he set himself to follow the path traced out by the great Afghan. His famous land revenue system was originally inaugurated by Sher Shah, as were many of his administrative reforms. From Sher Shah, too, he borrowed his policy of universal tolerance. He sought to emulate Sher Shah in the skill with which he laboured to conciliate antagonistic parties in the State, allowing fair play to all without distinction of creed.

Much as Akbar was indebted to Sher Shah he also owed a great deal to his ministers, Todar Mall, a Hindu, and Abul Fazl, a Muhammadan. Nevertheless, it was Akbar, and none but Akbar who created and consolidated the mighty Moghul empire. He was the architect even if he borrowed something of the design and built upon foundations already well and truly laid by a master hand. Without Akbar the work begun by Sher Shah would have gone for nought, the genius of Todar Mall, and rare qualities of Abul Fazl have proved as unprofitable as flowers that bloom in the desert. Akbar was the man of the age, and in India, as in Europe, the sixteenth century was pregnant with energy. It was an epoch-making era.

The soundness of Akbar's system, and its working quality are proved, not by the record of his reign alone, but by the still more reliable testimony of subsequent history. In spite of the weakness, vice and family feuds which marred the reigns of his successors, Jahangir and Jahan, the Moghul Empire was so solidly welded together as to remain intact until the advent of Aurangzib. By his fanatical zeal and narrow bigotry the last of the great Moghuls severed what the first, by means of a liberal-minded policy and a wise and humane tolerance, had united.

Possibly nothing about Akbar is more surprising nor more attractive than his versatility. He was as many sided as a finely-cut diamond. Regard him from what point one may he invariably appears in another light. Viewed as a soldier he was brave, dashing and extraordinarily active. As a sportsman he was fearless and more than commonly fortunate. Immeasurably superior as a statesman he ranks with the few really great monarchs the world has ever produced.

Padishah of the most conservative people on earth he yet consolidated his power by constant innovations. Abolishing old methods of counting he introduced solar reckoning and the Persian calendar. On current coin and in state documents he did away with the Kalimah, or Moslem profession of faith so obnoxious to Hindus. In its stead he substituted the simple formula 'Allahu Akbar,' 'God is most Great,' and 'Jallaha Jalahuhu,' 'Glorified be His Glory.' He discontinued the hated jizia, a tax on all not professing the tenets of Islam, and employed Hindus, Shiahs, and Sunnies without regard to creed.

With Akbar originated a species of feudal aristocracy the members of which were designated Mansabdars. In return for money payment, or lands, these undertock to provide the Imperial army with a stipulated number of men and elephants. Titles were not hereditary, and were on a sliding scale, an Amir of five thousand being a far more important personage than a commander of five hundred. The force was controlled by the Amir-ul-Umura, the Earl-Marshal of Hindustan.

So capable a ruler as Akbar was perforce a business man. Before proceeding to erect any building he required a detailed estimate, wherein every item was provided for. This he carefully perused, keeping a sharp look out that no margin was left for waste.

Akbar was too great a man to be orthodox. Among Muhammadans painting from life is regarded with disfavour as contrary to the divine commandments handed down by Moses. Uninfluenced by this religious prejudice Akbar was particularly fond of painting, and encouraged artists, taking the keenest interest in their work. He established a picture gallery and collected a number of artists. Every week the result of their efforts was laid out in front of him for criticism, censure or reward. In this way he caused Persian manuscripts to be finely illuminated, the margins decorated, and great care lavished upon the bindings. The walls of his sleeping apartment at Fatehpur Sikri, and of his tomb at Sikandarah, still further bear witness to his fondness for colour decoration.

'By His Majesty's command portraits are made of all the principal officers of the court which, being bound together form a thick volume wherein the past are kept in lively remembrance, and the present are insured immortality.'

As Akbar's many-sided character developed, and his intellect glowed more brightly, he took an ever-increasing interest in spiritual matters. Exponents of all creeds found him an attentive and respectful listener. He was tolerant of all but the intolerant. At Fatehpur Sikri a curious edifice, built round a massive central column, is the famous Ibadat Khana, or Hall of Worship, where priests and philosophers assembled on Friday nights for debate. Akbar took his seat in the centre enthroned on the capital of the pillar. In the encircling gallery Jesuit missionary, Brahmin priest, Jain, Buddhist, Shiah, Sunni, Parsi, Jogi, Fakir and Sadhu propounded their beliefs and unbeliefs in heated controversy.

The result of all this reasoning, arguing and religious research led the open-minded Emperor to the conclusion that no one faith was entitled to arrogate Divine Truth exclusively to itself. Having made this momentous discovery he generously desired to distribute the news abroad. Assisted by the clever and resourceful Abul Fazl, he accordingly proceeded to gather together those theories and beliefs which most appealed to him. With these pearls of wisdom, extracted from widely diverse oyster shells, he formed a collection which he presented to the world under the title of Tauhid-i-Ilhai, or Divine Monotheism. Apparently the ceremony of initiation was extremely simple. The convert removed his turban and held it on the palm of his hand. Bowing his head upon the Emperor's feet he repeated: 'I have cast away my presumption and selfishness, which were the cause of various evils, and am come a suppliant vowing to devote the remainder of my life in this world to the attainment of immortality.' At this Akbar raised the disciple, replaced the turban and pronounced the following benediction: 'My prayers are addressed to Heaven on your behalf, that your efforts may bear you from seeming existence to real existence.' Thereafter he was required to abstain from meat, and annually celebrate his birthday by feasting the poor and distributing alms.

Numerous miracles were attributed to Akbar. 'Many whose diseases are deemed incurable entreat him to breathe on them and are thereby restored to health,' records the Ain-i-Akbari. His converts, however, were few, and did not survive his reign.

The truly Catholic nature of Akbar's tastes is further illustrated in his choice of wives. Of his seven imperial consorts the first was daughter to the Sultan of Turkey, the third, Mariam-ul-Zamani, mother of Jahangir and of Prince Danial, was a daughter of Bihani Mall, Maharaja of Ambar (Jaipur) hence a Rajput and a worshipper of Rama. A fourth wife was likewise a Hindu, being a Princess of Marwar, and a fifth was an Armenian. That these matches were dictated by political considerations is proved by the Ain-i-Akbari; 'Great inconvenience is generally entailed by a number of women; but His Majesty, out of the abundance of his wisdom and prudence, has made it subservient to public advantage. By contracting marriages with the daughters of Hindu princes, and of other countries, he secures himself against insurrections at home, and forms powerful alliances abroad.'

Anecdotes relating to the private life of Akbar represent him as essentially good humoured, shrewd and devoted to his friends. It is told how he invariably drank the Ganges water and how, for superstitious reasons, he wore seven differently coloured suits during the week, so that he might always appear in the hues of the particular planets governing each day. ' His Majesty has introduced the custom of wearing two shawls, one under the other, which is a considerable addition to their beauty. . . . The rich dresses that are bestowed on the nobility on festivals are beyond description. Every quarter there are prepared one thousand Sirrapa, or complete costumes. They are tied up in separate bundles, each containing twenty-one. His Majesty is very fond of woollen stuffs, particularly shawls '.

Many instances are told of the lavish generosity displayed by the Great Moghul on all occasions. No needy person was ever denied assistance. ' For this purpose there is always a treasurer in waiting in the presence, and every beggar, who presents himself before His Majesty, has his necessities instantly relieved. . . . There are daily given away elephants, horses and many valuable articles to an astonishing amount.'

Twice a year the indigent received largess on a truly royal scale. This ceremony was known as Weighing the Royal Person. The first and most important took place on the Emperor's birthday, i.e. October 15th. Seating himself in a pair of scales Akbar was weighed twelve times against the following articles: gold, quicksilver, raw silk, artificial perfumes, musk, drugs, ghee, iron, rice, eight varieties of grain and salt. In addition sheep, goats and fowls were given away, the number distributed of each breed according with the age of the Badshah. Simultaneously large quantities of tame birds were set free.

The second weighing occurred in the Arabian month of Rejab when the Emperor sat in the scales and was weighed eight times. Similar ceremonies marked the birthdays of each of the princes.

Referring to his partiality for Yogis it is reported that, after retiring to his sleeping apartment in the Khwabgah, or House of Dreams, Fatehpur Sikri, a jogi, seated on a charpai, would be hauled up by ropes to the level of the imperial balcony. There, suspended in mid-air, for no man might pass the harem limits, the ascetic would converse with the Emperor far into the night.

All historians agree in describing the Emperor as an extraordinarily industrious man. He dispensed almost entirely with sleep, contenting himself with a brief interval of repose in the evening, and a second in the morning. The major portion of the night was devoted to conference with the various heads of departments, and great officials, generally regarding matters of state. Philosophers, Sufis and historians were also admitted. 'Three hours before dawn musicians of all nations are introduced to the presence, who recreate the assembly with vocal and instrumental melody. When it wants only about one hour of dawn, His Majesty prefers silence for his devotions.' At daybreak he appeared in a balcony for the Darshin, or showing ceremony. The nobility were assembled below, as were vast crowds 'without molestation from the mace bearers.' Whenever a court was to be held, it was announced by beat of kettledrum. Usually the Emperor took his seat on the throne in the Diwan-i-Am, or Great Hall of Justice, shortly after nine o'clock. Occasionally, however, this daily durbar was postponed until late in the afternoon or evening. Akbar ate once in twenty-four hours and then but sparingly. He had no appointed time for this meal, and only gave the cooks sixty minutes notice in which to prepare it. Never partial to meat his distaste for animal food increased as he grew older. Food was served to him in dishes of gold, silver, copper and china. Each was carefully sealed and wrapped up in a scarlet, or white cloth. Great precautions were taken to guard against poison. 'The servants of the presence again taste the victuals and then serve them up. When the table is ready His Majesty seats himself. The attendants place themselves round the table in a sitting posture. First the share of the Dervishes is set apart. His Majesty usually begins with milk or curds. After he has dined he says grace.' Akbar was punctilious with regard to his devotions, the set times for which were dawn, noon, sunset and midnight. He was fond of fruit. A large tray of it was invariably placed before him whenever he was about to indulge in wine, or opium. He was likewise much addicted to the use of perfumes. His body and head were frequently annointed with fragrant unguents. The presence chamber was constantly fumigated with incense burnt in gold and silver censers. Other scent was provided by flowers.

The Great Moghul venerated the sun and luminous heavenly bodies. This respect extended in a lesser degree to all lights. Special regulations were drawn up regarding those used in the palace. When the sun entered Aries (March 21) a shining onyx was exposed to its rays. No sooner was this gem thoroughly heated than fire was caught from it on a specially prepared piece of cotton. This divine spark was carefully tended throughout the year. The royal lamp-lighters, linkmen and cooks all availed themselves of it in the performance of their respective duties. 'Every afternoon, at one ghurry before sunset, His Majesty alights, if on horse-back. Should he be sleeping he is awakened. When the sun disappears the attendants light up twelve camphor candles, in twelve sticks of gold and silver, and bring them into the presence. A singer lifts up one of the candlesticks, sings a variety of sweet melodies and concludes with invoking blessings on His Majesty.'

These candlesticks were of diverse forms and extraordinary beauty. Some were many branched. The camphor candles were three yards in height and ornamented with flowers.

The interior of the fort was illuminated with torches affixed to poles having eight iron prongs each. During the first three nights of the new moon all eight flambeaux were lit. Thereafter they decreased one by one nightly until, on the tenth, when the moon shone brightly only one proved sufficient. From the twenty-first they lit a second and then a third, and so on until, by the thirtieth all eight prongs were again ablaze.

When the Emperor was in camp the site of the imperial tent was signalled by a great lantern set upon a pole 120 feet high, held in place by sixteen ropes.

In his private capacity Akbar seems to have been indulgent to excess. His son Jahangir speaks of his father's extreme love for his youngest daughter, who, according to her imperial brother, was a regular little spitfire and thoroughly spoiled.

Jahangir drew a graphic word picture of his father. By his description the Great Moghul was of middle height, lion-bodied, with an open chest and remarkably long arms and hands. His complexion was wheat-coloured and his eyes and brows black. On his left nostril was a very large mole, regarded by physiognomists to prognosticate great good fortune. His voice was clear and ringing. His speech was elegant and well chosen, and his countenance full of a 'God-like dignity,' while his manners were quite unlike those of other people. Such, in brief, was the external aspect of the man who, for forty-seven years, was the pivot around which the Indian Empire revolved.

The close of Akbar's long reign was saddened by the rebellion of his son Jahangir. This prince sought to seize the imperial treasury and marched against Agra, fortunately repenting before much mischief had been done. He sent to the Emperor imploring pardon. With his habitual generosity, Akbar forgave his son, but he never again entirely restored him to confidence.

Other sorrows were the tragic deaths of the Emperor's three much loved friends, Birbal—the Hindu poet-laureate and sometime Prime Minister, Faizi—the famous Muhammadan poet, and Abul Fazl, the historian, author of the Ain-i-Akbari or Institutes of Akbar, a work to which we owe the most minute details appertaining to the reign of this monarch. The death of his younger son, Prince Danial, who succumbed to intemperance, was the final blow to the already much-bereaved monarch. Under this last grief his failing health gave way and he died at Agra on the 17th of October, 1605, aged sixty-three years and one day.

He left his son a heritage of an assured empire that stretched eastwards from Kabul to Dakkha, and northwards from Ahmadnagar to Kashmir.

An assiduous student of history, that text-book of sovereigns, Akbar was a passionate advocate of all that was fine and beautiful. Great as were his military achievements they were eclipsed by the more lasting victories of peace won through a wise and sympathetic administration. He was a generous patron of art, architecture and letters, raising his reign to be a golden age in India. Enlightened, large-hearted, enthusiastic and of boundless sympathies such faults as he possessed were, as Ferishta says of him, 'but virtues carried to excess.'

ITINERARY

FIRST-DAY—FORENOON

Visit the Fort and Jama Masjid

THE FORT

Originally named Akbarabad, after its founder, the fort, or citadel, was commenced by Akbar A.D. 1565. By that date the Great Moghul had firmly established his supremacy in Hindustan, and had little to fear from outside attack, consequently the big red castle beside the Jumna is a fortified palace, rather than a structure planned more with a view to the stern business of war than the pleasures of peace.

The actual labour of building lasted eight years and furnised constant employment for over a thousand masons under the supervision of Kashim Khan, commander of the boats. The excellence of the work is proved by the fact that the citadel is still in a perfect state of preservation. No doubt, much of the credit for this is due to the peculiarly lasting quality of the masonry, which consists of red sandstone quarried at Fatehpur Sikri.

The fort, as it now stands, represents the combined efforts of three successive sovereigns. Designed and built by Akbar it was added to by Jahangir, while to Shah Jahan belong the white marble edifices which, if slightly out of keeping with the sterner character of the remainder, are gratefully accepted on account of their rare beauty.

As planned by Akbar the palace consisted of three courts characterized by stately porticoes, galleries and turrets, and adorned with rich paintings, carving and gilding, in places overlaid with panels of pure gold.

The first enclosure was surrounded by arcaded cloisters, and was occupied by the Imperial Guard. The second was reserved for the Omrahs and other ministers of state, to whom were assigned various offices wherein to transact public business. The third court was sacred to the seraglio. This was jealously screened by high walls. It contained the Emperor's apartments and was hung with the richest silks, Persian carpets, embroideries and kincobs, in a word all that the wealth of Ind could lavish of beautiful and rare.

Beyond lay the king's garden, an earthly paradise of brightest colour and deepest shade. Fountains and water channels cooled the scented air. Birds sang from the tree tops and butterflies fluttered from flower to flower in an atmosphere redolent of perfume and of song.

Between the castle and the river was a maidan, where elephants were exercised and wild beast fights took place, watched by the Emperor and the court. This was a form of sport to which the Moghuls were much addicted.

A wide square separated the palace from the town. In this, large bodies of troops were constantly encamped. Their bright trappings, shining armour and brilliant ensigns added much to the splendours surrounding the Emperor.

Mandelso, who visited Agra in 1638, spoke of the palace as the grandest object he had ever beheld. He describes it as enclosed by a high freestone wall and a broad ditch, across which draw-bridges connected with each gate. At the further end of the inner court was a pavilion supported by silver pillars. Beyond lay the presence chamber, where a small row of gold columns formed a balustrade about the throne, described as a massive divan of solid gold studded with glittering gems. No doubt this was the famous Peacock

Throne constructed by order of Shah Jahan. Immediately above, was a marble recess in the wall where the great Moghul appeared daily, at a stated time, to hear complaints and redress grievances. None but princes of the blood might pass the golden balustrade.

Mandelso also mentions eight large treasure vaults filled with gold, silver and precious stones, and speaks of a tower roofed with sheets of gold.

Considerable changes in the interior of the palace were effected by Shah Jahan. The present arrangement is the result, although further modifications have been introduced since, notably after the British took possession.

OUTER WALLS

Abul Fazl describes Akbar's citadel as comprising four gateways, 'which open the doors of wealth and prosperity on the four quarters of the world.' The fortifications consist of an outer and an inner wall. About the former, which is a mile and a half in circuit, was dug a paved ditch thirty-five feet deep and thirty feet wide, a work generally attributed to Aurangzib. Above it the curtain rises some forty feet, and includes fifteen bastions and towers. Drawbridges connect with the main, or Delhi Gate, in the northern portion of the west wall, and the South Gate, to east of the south wall. To west of the latter entrance the head of a horse, carved in red sandstone, may be seen protruding above the soil. The body is said to be rough and unfinished. According to legend it was the charger of Amar Singh Rathor, the Maharaja of Jodhpur. At a tilting match in the courtyard of the Diwan-i-Am, Amir Singh slew Salabhat Khan, the imperial chief treasurer. For this he was instantly slain, as drawing a sword in the Emperor's presence constituted a capital offence. His charger escaped and leaping the southern rampart was turned into stone. The incident is attributed to 1644, at which epoch Shah Jahan was in power. Beyond again is a square tomb of red sandstone. This box shaped monument bears a marble tablet inscribed: 'Sacred to the memory of Sittanah Beghum, the faithful and affectionate friend and, companion of Lieut. Shairp, who died on December 3, 1804.

Before the Jumna was depleted by the present canal system, the river washed the eastern ramparts during the monsoon. On this side a covered way connected the postern of the Samman Burj, or Jasmine Tower with the water gate of the outer wall, where stood the bathing ghats sacred to the ladies of the harem. These were demolished in 1837 when the strand was constructed. Tradition relates that the time honoured custom of burying criminals, with other propitiatory human sacrifices, under the foundations of buildings, was duly observed by Akbar when erecting his fort. Colour is lent to this by a statement that in 1857 European refugees in the citadel discovered skeletons when searching for treasure trove beneath the Khas Mahal. The practice arose through the desire to appease the earth goddess. Furthermore the spirits of those buried alive were credited with the power of guarding the edifices under which they lay entombed, and of warding off demons and other evil influences.

INNER WALL

The inner line of defences, like the outer, is faced with blocks of red sandstone over a rubble hearting largely composed of sand. It is similarly loopholed for musketry and displays imposing gateways embattlemented ramparts and banquettes, excepting where palaces, and similar edifices overlook the river. In the days or the Great Moghuls the Jumna was a crowded watercourse gay with richly painted, carved and gilded royal barges, light craft belonging to the nobility, ferries and lumbering country boats laden with produce and merchandise of all descriptions. Akbar paid particular attention to his fleet, hence the Ain-i-Akbari records: 'Every part of the Empire abounds in boats. His Majesty has had some pleasure boats built with convenient apartments. The head of each is made to resemble some animal. On others are floating markets and flower gardens. Some are used for the transportation of elephants and some for use in sieges. . . . An active resolute man is appointed to watch the rivers. He settles everything relative to the ferries, regulates tonnage and provides travellers with boats. Those unable to pay are ferried over gratis but no one is allowed to swim across.'

The inner curtain of the citadel is about forty feet higher than the outer, and possesses sixteen bastions. Formerly a platform projected from the south face of the wall, between the Bangali Burj and the turret to west of it. This served for public executions. In spite of their height the fortifications lose considerably in effect owing to the flatness of the site, and the houses which now crowd around in close proximity.

MAIN ENTRANCE

Akbar's citadel lies immediately south of Agra Fort Station. The principal entrance is the north, or Delhi Gate, reached by a metalled road and drawbridge. It is guarded by a projecting bastioned barbicon. From it a steep paved way winds up between high walls to the celebrated Hathi Pol, or Elephant Gate, so called because of two large stone elephants, which, with their riders, used to occupy the platforms to right and left of the arch. They commemorated Akbar's capture of Chittoor in 1568, and bore life sized figures of those immortal Rajput warriors, Jai Mal and Fathur. The English merchant mariner, William Finch, who visited Agra in 1612, writes of the main entrance : 'Over against the great portal is the Cazi, his seat of Chief Justice in matters of law, and by it two or three mortars, very great, of cast brass. Beyond these two gateways' (the outer wall and barbicon gateways collectively styled the Delhi Darwaza owing to being connected by an arcade) 'you pass a second gate, over which are two Rajas in stone, who were slain in the King's Darbar before the King's very eyes for being overbold in speech.' These statues were destroyed by Aurangzib, whose fanatical zeal led him to literally interpret the commandment of Moses prohibiting graven images.

The Naubhat Khana, or Music Gallery was situated in the Hathi Pol. From the upper part the imperial kettledrums announced the arrival and departure of the Emperor and played during state functions. The gate also contained a guard-house and quarters for military officers.

THE MOTI MASJID

The old Moghul road led direct to the Diwan-i-Am, or Hall of Public Audience. Subsequent alterations have materially affected this original plan. Now the route from the Elephant Gate runs north-east for about a thousand feet, through a somewhat cheerless tract to the Moti Masjid, or Pearl Mosque, a lofty building of white marble visible from afar. Considering how conspicuous the sanctuary is, it is astonishing how it escaped damage during the various attacks to which the fort has been subjected. In common with other marble additions it is the work of Shah Jahan. It cost three lakhs of rupees and took seven years to build. The site was formerly occupied by older edifices sacrificed to make space for it.

Steps and an imposing gate admit to the courtyard, wherein stand a sundial and the essential hauz, or tank for ablutions. The unbroken whiteness comes as a surprise after the prevailing red glow outside. Three graceful white domes rise above the Mosque which is 142 feet long and fifty-six feet deep. Triple rows of seven arches spring from great pillars of square design. At either side carved screens of beautifully fretted and pierced marble safeguard the privacy of the harem enclosures.

The floor is delicately inlaid with lines of rich blue and pale yellow marble, the only touches of colour in the building. These divide it off into five hundred and seventy *masalan*, or prayer spaces for men. The remaining ninety were reserved for the Begams and other ladies of the court. The Mihrabs, or recesses in the main wall to west, were originally open, after the manner of windows, to allow the Faithful a view of the sun setting in all his splendour where Mecca is. Muhammadans must ever turn towards their Holy City when engaged in devotions. To right of the central Mihrab is the Mimbar, or pulpit. According to tradition an immense pearl of wondrous size and lustre was suspended from the ceiling by a golden chain. A boldly written Persian inscription runs across the facade. It states that the temple was commenced by Shah Jahan in 1648 and finished in 1655. The lettering is of black slate, marble being too brittle for the purpose.

The roof commands a fine view of the Taj Mahal to east and wide winding river. On the further bank rises yet another splendid mauseleum, that of Itmad-ud-Daulah, father-in-law to Jahangir. Away to the north-west the mighty Akbar sleeps in the garden of Bihishtabad at Sikandara. Below the horizon, to south-west lies Fatehpur Sikri, once proud city of victory.

During the Sepoy Mutiny of 1857, the Pearl Mosque was used as a European hospital.

THE DARSHINI DARWAZA

A little beyond the Moti Masjid an inclined passage runs down to an old gateway known as the Darshini Darwaza, before reaching which it passes the site of an ancient palace. Finch mentions this gate as the spot to which the Emperor repaired daily at sunrise for the Darshin, or showing ceremony. It formed part of Akbars private apartments. Here he was in the habit of gazing out at the growing splendour of the eastern sky. As the sun appeared above the horizon the Great Moghul bowed low in prayer. Turning from its dazzling brilliancy he bent his eyes upon the courtyard beneath, where nobles and people were assembled to make obeisance to him, their newly risen sun. Finch witnessed the ceremony in Jahangir's time. As such he describes all present as falling on their faces and kissing the ground. 'Right under this place, whence he looks out, is a kind of scaffold whereon the nobles stand.' Finch further states that Jahangir returned here at noon to witness fights between various wild beasts specially trained for the purpose, notably elephants and tigers, lions and buffaloes. This sport was spoken of as a *tamashah*. Deer were turned loose to become the prey of leopards. Gazelle were abandoned to the tender mercies of birds of prey. The programme was varied once a week by the shedding of human blood. On Tuesdays it was the Emperor's custom to judge prisoners and witness their immediate execution. It is only fair to state that no killing of man or animal was permitted on Friday, the Muhammadan sabbath, which the Emperor spent in the harem.

Under Akbar these animal fights appear to have been less frequent. The beasts and birds used were deer, buffaloes, bulls, rams, goats and cocks. Wagers were laid. The animals belonging to the Emperor were pitted against those of the nobles. According to Abul Fazl, 'These battles were fought at night, on the fourteenth day of the moon, in front of the palace.'

The Darshini Darwaza leads out into the east enclosure depicted by Finch as 'a fair court extending along the river.' During the mutiny of 1857 it was converted into a bazaar for the use of refugees. In Moghul times the Water Gate is believed to have been reserved for the harem. This area, near the Samman Burj, was the recreation ground of the court ladies, and was probably laid out as a beautiful garden.

THE MINAR BAZAAR

After leaving the Moti Masjid the main road throws off a branch to right in the direction of the Minar Bazaar. Built of red sandstone the old time mart dates from Akbar and is surrounded by rows of open shops. Here merchants sat crosslegged, or knelt, Persian fashion, in front of their wares, their hubble-bubbles beside them, and in their eyes the mingled look, at once defensive and inviting, of the pedlar who has wares to sell, but at his price, not yours.

THE GREAT COURT

Originally the Akbari Darwaza was the principal entrance of the Great Court of the palace. It pierces the centre of the northern wall. Finch describes it as guarded by chains. Here all but the Emperor and his sons were required to alight. Inside stretches an open plain, 600 feet by 370 feet, grass planted and shaded with nims. Around it high brick walls rise above arcaded cloisters, once occupied by officers of the Imperial Guard. The roofs were crowded with spectators at all court functions. After the British occupation these galleries and rooms served as gunsheds. The east side is dominated by the Diwan-i-Am. To north of it a gate leads into the Zenana Minar Bazaar of famous memory. To south of it is a closed portal admitting to the Anguri Bagh. The centre of the southern side displays yet another lofty stone portico. During the mutiny two of its doors were bricked up. They connected with the vast labyrinth of subterranean passages and apartments, wherewith the foundations of the citadel are honey-combed to a considerable depth.

On the lawn the eye is caught by the tomb of the Hon'ble J. R. Colvin, Lieut.-Governor of the North-West Provinces, who died in the fort during the troubled days of 1857. Another prominent object is the large baoli, or well, eighty feet deep, and twenty-six feet in diameter, lined with immense blocks of red sandstone. It possesses steps and was worked by bullocks.

DIWAN-I-AM

The Hall of Public Audience occupies the centre of the eastern face of the courtyard. Composed of red sandstone, it measures 201 feet from north to south and projects sixty-seven feet westward from the wall of the Macchi Bhawan. This great pavilion is open in the front and at the sides, and is raised upon a plinth, some three or four feet high, approached by a flight of six steps. The interior dimensions are 192 feet by 62 feet. The flat roof is supported by three aisles of nine bays. Elaborate arches spring from Saracenic pillars, coated with white stucco and gilded. Quadruple pillars mark the corners, and fourteen double columns stretch along each open face. Originally, kiosks, or other edifices seem to have stood upon the terraced roof, which displays brackets holding up a dripstone surmounted by a plain parapet.

The hall is backed by a wall. Midway this opens to form a recess, or balcony a few feet above the ground, protected by a carved railing and triple arches of white marble. The walls of the recess are similarly of white marble and are beautifully inlaid with mosaic flowers in semi-precious stones. The decorations are attributed to Jahan. Below, on the floor, is a baithak, or marble platform raised upon four legs. This was originally enclosed by a silver railing.

THE IMPERIAL BALCONY

It was in the imperial balcony, known as the Jharokah or Judgment Seat, that the Emperor appeared daily to hear petitions and generally devote himself to the welfare of his subjects. None but nobles of the highest rank ever penetrated the silver balustrade of the baithak, on to which they stepped to hand petitions to the Badshah, or King of Kings. In those days of bribery and corruption it is easy to imagine what large sums had to be expended by a suppliant before his petition reached the august presence. To further the ends of justice, and defeat the greed of his entourage, Jahangir caused a chain to be suspended from the citadel. This hung down to the ground. It communicated with a peel of golden bells near the Judgment Seat. By this device he intended every suiter to personally inform him of his appeal, without being first driven to cross the itching palm of some influential courtier with gold.

Finch describes a royal darbar as held by Jahangir: 'A little further you enter a rail into a more inward court within which none but the King's Addis, and men of sort were admitted under pain of smacking by the porter's cudgels, which they lay on without respect of persons. . . '. The red rail is three steps higher than the place where the rest stand. Men are placed by officers. There are others to keep order. In the midst, right before the king, standeth an officer with his master hangman, accompanied by forty others of the same profession, with badges on their shoulders, and others with whips. Here the king heareth causes some hours every day. He then departs to his House of Prayer.'

The open court in front was the tilting ground. Troops and the royal elephants, horses, camels, bullocks and mules were in turn paraded on specified days. Terry, who also visited Agra during Jahangir's reign, describes the throne as ascended by steps plated with silver and ornamented with four silver lions, 'spangled with jewels,' which supported a canopy of pure gold.

To right and left of the throne recess are windows screened with pierced and fretted white marble. There are eight in all, two large and six small. Originally the interstices were filled in with brilliantly coloured glass manufactured in Delhi. Behind these the harem ladies could see without being seen.

The imperial balcony is entered from the back whence it communicates with the Macchi Bhawan and Zanana buildings.

Bernier, the French physician attached to the Court of Aurangzib, gives a graphic description of the scene daily enacted in the Diwan-i-Am. Seated cross-legged on his gorgeous throne, in the marble recess, the Emperor presented a dazzling picture, arrayed in all the splendour of his matchless jewels. Brilliantly clad attendants fanned him gently with long-handled fans, while others, armed with peacock feather switches, kept off insects, the fly and ubiquitous mosquito being no respecter of persons. Near to the throne, and only less magnificent than the central figure, stood princes of the blood. Below, in the hall, were grouped the omerahs, the flower of the nobility. Further off, and separated by a silver railing, were lesser dignitaries, and, beyond again came the waiting crowd of supplicants. All, whether Rajas or beggars, adopted the same attitude of abject humility and most profound respect.

When the proceedings threatened to grow monotonous, horses and elephants, from the imperial stables, were paraded before the Emperor. Glancing keenly over their accoutrements he satisfied himself that the animals were immaculately groomed and in good condition. When the British occupied the fort, early in the nineteenth century, they bricked up the sides and front of the Diwan-i-Am and used it as an armoury until 1870, when the contents were transferred to Allahabad. It was restored in honour of the King-Emperor Edward VII who, as Prince of Wales, visited Agra in January 1876. A grand Darbar was held in it on January 12, 1807, when Lord Minto invested His Highness Habibulla Khan, the late Amir of Afghanistan, with the order of the Bath.

INNER MINAR BAZAAR

The gateway on the left of the Great Court gives access to a small private bazaar used by the ladies of the harem. The fair purchasers looked down from the marble balcony, while merchants unfolded their wares on the ground below.

Sometimes the place was converted into a play-ground. The wives and daughters of the nobles acted the part of merchants, while the Emperor and the Begams did their best to drive hard bargains with the pretty pedlars. All the tricks of the trade were cleverly imitated, and many a merry laugh ensued, especially when a particularly lively controversy ended by the saleswoman receiving a piece of gold.

This playing at shop originated with Akbar. Under him one day a month was set apart as a public holiday. The great festival of the year was Nau Roz, or New Year's Day celebrated when the sun enters the sign of Aries on March 21. Feasting continued for nineteen days, immense sums of money were distributed and gifts and honours bestowed. For three nights public illuminations were ordered on a lavish scale. The date of the monthly festivals varied. That of April fell on the third. In May, the sixth, was a general holiday, in June the thirteenth, in July the seventh and so on.

The Khushroz, or Day of Diversion was associated with the Inner Minar Bazaar. Of this custom the Ain-i-Akbari records: 'His Majesty gives this name to the ninth day after the festival of each month, and thereon assembles his court. Upon this occasion the wives of merchants hold a market, where they expose for sale the manufactures of every country, at their respective shops. The women of the Harem, and others of good repute, resort thither and carry on a large traffic to the mutual satisfaction of all parties. His Majesty is also there in disguise. By this means he learns the prices of different articles of merchandize, and hears what is said of the state of the empire, and the characters of the officers of government. When the female fair is over, another is set on foot for the men. His Majesty and the courtiers come and purchase. At this time every man may represent his particular grievances, without the intervention of any one; when the injured never fail to obtain redress and the offenders are punished. A Treasurer and Munshiff are appointed to this department, that the merchants may receive immediate payment.'

It would be interesting to know whether the Emperor attended the women's bazaar in feminine disguise. Presumably he must have done so as men were not admitted. In later reigns the quaint old custom seems to have sadly degenerated and to have earned an evil reputation for license. This led to the Rajput's introducing a special clause into one of their treaties. It stipulated that the vassals of Boondi should be exempted from the obligation of sending their wives, or female relatives to take a stall in the Minar Bazaar, at the palace on the festival of Nau Roz.

NAGINA MASJID

Overlooking the south-west angle of the Inner Minar Bazaar is a beautiful little mosque of white marble. Known as the Nagina Masjid, it was exclusively reserved for the ladies of the zenana.

It is generally ascribed to Aurangzib who is said to have built it about 1658. Apparently it occupies the site of an earlier sandstone structure, which stood on a level with the first floor of the Macchi Bhawan, whence the Mosque is reached by a door in the south wall.

Stairs lead up to a marble paved court enclosed on three sides. The fourth to west, opens into the Mosque, which is flanked by two smaller courts, likewise marble-paved. In addition they are screened by pierced marble. All three are divided into *masalan*, or prayer spaces with fine lines of black slate. The smaller of these spaces were for children.

The sanctuary is raised on a plinth and consists of two aisles of triple bays conspicuous for graceful arches and a beautiful vaulted and cusped roof, surmounted by three domes, and eight pinnacles tipped with glittering gilt spikes. A door to south admits to a small chamber, where water was heated. From here, a second door leads into the balcony of the Inner Minar Bazaar.

To north-west of the Gem Mosque is a small roo m. In this prescribed space, tradition avers that the Emperor Jahan was kept in durance vile by his undutiful son, Aurangzib. A little screened window is pointed out as the place through which the once splendid, and prodigal monarch looked out daily to receive the salute of the guard posted in the great court below. The Nagina Masjid is believed to have originally connected with the Pearl Mosque by a covered way, which passed over the gate of the Inner Minar Bazaar.

Conflicting views are expressed regarding the treatment accorded the captive Emperor. Manucci, the Venetian, was in Agra when Aurangzib entered the city at the head of his victorious army. The conqueror encamped in the garden of Nur Manzil (Palace of Light) the site of which is now included in cantonments. Manucci describes how Aurangzib prevailed upon Shah Jahan to yield up the keys of the fort. At this he despatched his confidential eunuch, I'tibar Khan, to confine the old Emperor in the harem. His eldest, and passionately loved daughter, the beautiful Jahanara Begam, was imprisoned with him, as were the rest of the women, some two thousand in all. The second daughter, Roshanara Begam, who had espoused her brother Aurangzib's cause throughout, was brought forth in triumph. 'Then I'tibar Khan caused many gates and wickets to be built up, posting here and there harsh women guardians, in such a way that Shah Jahan could neither speak, nor write to any one outside, nor step beyond the door of his harem to enjoy a stroll in the garden without the eunuch's leave.'

CHITOOR GATES

Near the south-east side of the corridor-enclosed court of the Inner Minar Bazaar, stand the famous Gates of Chitoor. These are of handsomely wrought metal, and are trophies of war brought to Agra in 1568, after Akbar's capture of the celebrated Rajput stronghold. They lead into the Macchi Bhawan, but are rarely opened.

MANDIH RAJA RATAN

Such is the local name applied to the quadrangle, enclosed by arcaded cloisters, which lies east of the Chitoor Gates. On the southern face inscribed stone tablets state that Raja Ratan Nain Sukh, the Faujdar, or General of Maharaj Pirthi

Indar, erected it as residence for himself in 1768, during the Jat occupation of the fort, which extended from 1761 until 1774. As the style is Saracenic the probability is that he merely took up his quarters in an existing Moghul edifice. Havell identifies it as a Hindu temple.

MACCHI BHAWAN

The Macchi Bhawan, or Fish Palace, derives its name from the fish, which used to fill the central tank of the courtyard. The beautiful buildings, wherewith it is surrounded, were sadly mutilated, and even entirely destroyed by those Governors-General, Lord Hastings (1813-23) and Lord W. Bentinck (1828-36). The former removed and sent home much of the beautiful ornamentation as a gift to the Prince Regent. The latter tore down exquisite marble screens and other masterpieces of decorative art. He also demolished a wonderful pavilion of green marble, which stood on the east side above the Hamman Shahi, or Emperor's Baths. The fragments he put up to public auction and sold for building materials. But for the low prices realized, the Taj Mahal would have shared the same fate.

The Macchi Bhawan lies behind the Diwan-i-Am. It communicates with the throne recess by means of steps and a door, and consists of a red sandstone courtyard measuring about 164 feet from north to south, and some 132 feet from east to west. This space is now grass planted and dominated by a large nim tree. In the splendid days of Shah Jahan it was laid out in geometrically designed flower beds bordered with white marble. The same royal stone fashioned fountains, water channels and fish tanks. These were all carried off to Dig in Bharatpur, by Suraj Mal. With them he adorned his palace garden, where they may be seen in excellent preservation to this day.

Arcaded cloisters of the prevailing sandstone run round the square. They are provided with a broad horizontal ledge and substantial brackets designed to support the poles of an awning. The verandah is narrowest on the east side, and admits to somewhat gloomy rooms under the Throne Terrace, whence dark passages communicate with the Sammam Burj.

The centre of the north side is pierced by the Macchi Bhawan gate, the upper storey of which contains two rooms. In the south-east corner, on a white marble mural tablet is inscribed: 'In grateful commemoration of the services rendered to posterity by the Hon'ble Sir John Strachey, G.C.S.I., to whom, not forgetting the enlightened sympathy and kindly care of others, India is mainly indebted for the rescued and preserved beauty of the Taj Mahal, and other famous monuments of the ancient art and history of these provinces formerly administered by him, this tablet is placed by order of his friend, the Earl of Lytton, Viceroy and Governor-General of India, A.D. 1880'.

MINA NASJID

To right a few steps lead up to the Mina, or Heavenly Mosque, once the private chapel of the Emperor. Cased with white marble, it is very small, merely measuring twenty-two feet by thirteen feet. Floor spaces admit of eighteen worshippers. It faces a court twenty-two feet square. Stairs ascend to the roof.

THE THRONE TERRACE

To east of the garden, a flight of steps mounts to a broad terrace overlooking the river. Tradition asserts that it was once marble paved, and inlaid with coloured mosaic. Above it rose a beautiful white marble baradari, or pavilion carried off by the Jat leader, Suraj Mal, in the eighteenth century.

The terrace is 116 feet long by 82 feet deep, and is protected by a low-carved rail of white marble. Great iron rings attached to the floor served for a tent or canopy.

THE GREAT WHITE THRONE

In the centre of the terrace, two thrones face each other. The one to west is of white marble, and consists of a rectangular slab raised upon four legs. It is reputed to have been the seat of the Court Justice, at which epoch it was enclosed by a shallow rail. Tradition further avers that it was a favourite seat of Shah Jahan, whence he amused himself by casting a fishing line into the tank below.

THE GREAT BLACK THRONE

The second throne is black. It is carved out of a single block of slate and measures ten feet seven inches, by nine feet ten inches and has a thickness of six inches. Four octagonal legs raise it sixteen inches above the ground. An inscription runs round the edge describing Prince Salim (afterwards the Emperor Jahangir) as Shah Salim. The date given is 1602. At that epoch the heir to the Great Moghul was an open rebel. He had defied his father, Akbar, by assuming imperial functions at Allahabad, in which city he held his court. Shortly afterwards, he came to Agra, sued for pardon and was forgiven. Probably he brought the throne from Allahabad upon the death of Akbar in 1605, as a second inscription records his accession in that year, under the title of Nur-ud-Din Muhammad Jahangir.

The slab is cracked right across, and stained dull red in two places. The tale runs that the split occurred when Raja Jawahir Singh of Bharatpur attempted to mount the great black throne upon the death of his father, Suraj Mal, at Delhi in 1763. Jawahir Singh was living in Agra Fort at the time. At his desecrating touch, the slate broke and spurted blood. The omen was of sinister portent. In 1766, he was murdered close by the scene of the incident.

HAMMAM SHAHI

The King's Baths are situated at the northern end of the throne terrace. Originally the earthen floors were paved with marble and mosaic, and the stucco-coated walls resplendent with gorgeous colour decorations overlaid with gold leaf. Copper pipes formed part of an elaborate system whereby water was abundantly supplied to the suite of vaulted bath rooms. Brilliantly hued glass filled the interstices of the white marble window screens looking out on to the river. On the plinth, at the southern end of the Hammam, stood the peerless green marble pavilion demolished by Lord W. Bentinck. Its position and design are shown in old pictures.

DIWAN-I-KHAS

Such is the name given to the beautiful white marble pavilion at the south extremity of the throne terrace. It constituted the Hall of Private Audience. An inscription, in the form of a Persian chronogram, states that it was erected in 1637, the eleventh year of Jahan's reign. Allusion is also made to the Chain of Justice. This was attached to a bell in the Diwan-i-Khas, and probably extended to the carousal of the Diwan-i-Am. By pulling it a suppliant could obtain immediate access to the presence, a device originally introduced by Jahangir.

The Audience Chamber stands on a plinth beautifully carved about the edge, and consists of two halls. The outer measures seventy-three feet by thirty-three feet and the inner forty feet by twenty-six feet. Large rings provide for silken awnings. Saracenic arcades display twelve-sided pillars, exquisitely chiselled and inlaid with many coloured flowers in semi-precious stones, such as jade, lapis lazuli, agate and others.

The inner chamber is remarkable for its marble window screens. The dadoes are splendidly carved in a series of panels. Further embellishment takes the form of mosaic. Gold and silver lamps hung from hooks in the ceiling of the flat roof.

It was in the Diwan-i-Khas that the court assembled every evening. The Emperor attached considerable importance to these nightly durbars. Absence was construed as an act of *lese majeste*, and severely punished. Bernier describes the Great Moghul on such occasions as seated in a chair with his Omrahs, or grandees grouped about him. Here his officers presented their reports and transacted all important state affairs. Rajas and Ambassadors were received in private audience.

When the Amir of Afghanistan was invested with the Order of the Bath, in 1907, the Diwan-i-Khas was converted into a supper room. The deep bullet hole, in its eastern face, was made by Lord Lake's cannon in 1803.

SAMMAN BURJ

From the Diwan-i-Khas a doorway leads to the Samman Mahal, or Jasmine Palace, so called because of the flowers, in delicate mosaic, wherewith it is decorated. Although popularly attributed to Jahan the building probably dates from Jahangir, more especially as Nur Jahan is said to have designed the inlay work during her three years' sojourn at Agra, after her marriage to the Emperor, in 1611. Later on Jahan occupied the Jasmine Palace with his beautiful wife, the lady for whom he built the Taj. During the mutiny of 1857, military and civil officers were quartered in it with their families. It comprises a court, forty-four feet by thirty-three feet, faced by an entrance hall to south, flanked by two rooms. This hall measures twenty-eight feet by eighteen feet. The walls bear traces of brilliant colour decoration and gilding. The quadrangle is paved with marble octagons where the game of pachisi, a species of backgammon, is said to have been played by the Emperor and Begams. It is further averred that gaily dressed nautch girls served as pieces moving gracefully from square to square as directed. The boundary wall to west displays holdfasts for an awning. Here stood the exquisite marble verandah demolished by Lord Hastings, who despatched the fragments to England. The pierced white marble screens to north were damaged by cannon shot and subsequently repaired.

The roof supports the famous Samman Burj, or Jasmine Tower, an octagonal pavilion surmounted by an open upper storey crowned by a gilt cupola. Here Mumtaz-i-Mahal spent the last year of her life. In this beautiful pavilion of many memories Jahan, the captive Emperor, breathed his last in December, 1666. With him was Jahanara Began, his devoted daughter. His dying gaze was fixed upon the Taj Mahal, where he was so soon to join the wife, for whom he had built the most peerless tomb of all ages.

The tower commands an extensive panorama. To south it looks across Macdonald Park. A glimpse is caught of Queen Victoria's statue and of Circuit House beyond.

THE ANGURI BAGH

The Anguri Bagh, or Vinery, occupies a large courtyard to south of the Macchi Bhawan, and was the garden of the Khas Mahal. It extends 220 feet north and south by 169 feet east and west. Three sides are encircled by the usual arcaded cloisters, and were inhabited by the harem. They date from

Akbar and are two storied and built of red sandstone. Four straight paths radiate from a raised central platform of white marble, twenty-six feet square, and two and a half feet deep, provided with a tank and fountains. The spaces between are intersected by ridges of red sandstone which form flower beds of geometrical design. The soil is reputed extraordinarily rich and is said to have been brought from Kashmir. Stone posts and latticed screens supported grape vines. The parterres were gay with blossoms, brightly coloured and fragrant, as well as rare plants.

KHAS MAHAL

A raised marble terrace dominates the eastern end of the Anguri Bagh. Here stand the three white marble pavilions forming the Khas Mahal (Private Palace) or Aramgarh (Abode of Rest). In this most beautiful part of the fort, the imperial ladies had their apartments. There is evidence that the site was occupied by earlier buildings erected by Akbar, and demolished by Jahan, in order to make room for his marble additions.

The central edifice looks on to a court measuring 96 feet by 112 feet. Pierced marble screens, some eight feet high, divide it from side courts extending eighty-eight feet by sixty-two feet to right and left. The middle hall is believed to have been a species of drawing-room whither Jahan repaired daily to converse with the princesses and principal ladies of the harem. Elaborate carving decorates pillars and arches. Originally the scheme of ornamentation included richly gilt and coloured poppy and other designs. Part of the ceiling has been renovated accordingly. Shallow wall recesses are said to have framed portraits of all the Moghul Emperors from Timur down. The escape channel of the tank in the chief court is a remarkably fine example of zigzag inlay-

The five fountains and thirty-two jets were fed from tanks on the roof of the Jahangiri Mahal.

The northern pavilion is reputed to have been the residence of Roshanara Begam, the second of Jahan's daughters, and the favourite sister of Aurangzib. It consists of a central chamber between two smaller ones. One of the fretted window screens was of wood. This was replaced by marble, in 1907, and entailed an expenditure of Rs. 289. The little vaults in the walls have a pretty story told of them. Occasionally the Emperor dropped a jewel into one surreptitiously. The fortunate finder was thereby entitled to be his companion for the day.

Princess Jahanara, popularly known as the Begam Sahib, occupied the southern pavilion with the bright gilt roof.

CHATRI OF RAJA JAWANIR SINGH

This consists of a miniature carving in bas-relief of a pavilion, and lamp niche in red sandstone, on the vertical face of the basement of the Khas Mahal, below the marble screen protecting the west side of the south court. It marks the site of the murder of the Jat Raja assassinated in the fort, in 1766. Guides point it out to visitors on the way to the Shah Jahan Mahal.

TAI KHANA

Most of the entrances to the bewildering labyrinth of underground stairways, passages and apartments, used by the court in hot weather, have been closed. Steps still lead from the south of the Khas Mahal to a few subterranean chambers. The first of these is said to have been the guard-room of the Nubian women warders employed to watch the zenana. Further on a grim story is told of a dark apartment, its ceiling crossed by an ornamental beam pierced by a hole above a black aperture. Here refractory members of the harem are said to have been hanged, and their bodies dropped into the shaft below whence they were swept away by the broad waters of the Jumna. Picturesque though the legend is, with its lurid appeal to the imagination, it belongs to the realm of fiction. As a matter of fact the beam was not a gallows, nor the rope a halter, but a prosaic contrivance for hauling water from the depths of an immense well.

That drastic punishment was meted out to offending ladies is abundantly proved. A striking instance is furnished by the case of poor Anakali (Pomegranate Blossom). The Emperor Akbar surprised this beautiful favourite exchanging amorous glances in a mirror with his son and heir, Prince Salim, afterwards Jahangir Shah. He immediately caused her to be buried alive on the spot now covered by the great white mausoleum to her memory in Lahore, a monument erected by her remorseful lover upon succeeding to the throne.

The Ain-i-Akbari records the rules governing the imperial harem, an enclosure of such immense extent as to contain a room for each woman to a number exceeding five thousand. 'They are divided into companies and a proper employment assigned to each individual. Over every company a woman is appointed Darogha. One is selected to command the whole, in order that the offices of the harem may be conducted with the same regularity, and good government as the other departments of State. Every one receives a salary equal to her merits. Ladies of the first quality receive from Rs. 1,610 down to Rs. 1,028. At the grand gate is stationed a Mushriff to take accounts of the harem expenditure.

The inside of the harem is guarded by women, of whom the most trustworthy are posted about the gate of the royal apartments. Immediately outside the gate watch the eunuchs, and, at a proper distance, the Rajputs. Besides all these precautions, His Majesty depends on his own vigilance.'

Manucci describes Jahan as protected by an Amazon guard of fierce Tartar women, expert in the use of bows and arrows, and ready to fight to the death in his defence.

SHISH MAHAL

The Shish Mahal, or Palace of Mirrors, is reached through a passage leading from the north-east corner of the Anguri Bagh. It lies under the Diwan-i-Khas and is Moorish in style. Walls and ceilings are spangled with innumerable fragments of looking glass set into gorgeously gilt and coloured stucco. Originally the floor was marble paved. The suite served as Turkish baths and dressing rooms to the harem.

SHAH JAHAN MAHAL

Such is the name applied to that part of Jahangir's Palace subsequently adapted by Shah Jahan to his particular tastes and requirements, hence the brick work additions, coated with plaster, to what had been a purely sandstone edifice. Later on, under British rule, several of the best rooms were utilized as a museum, until 1875, when the Archæological Society of Agra tranferred their exhibits to Allahabad. The front corridor opens on to the marble screened court to south of the Khas Mahal. The arcaded facade is divided into five bays by pillars and engrailed arches. Behind are various rooms characterised by lavishly gilt and coloured dadoes. The central chamber is pointed out as Jahangir's bed-room. Here the Hon'ble J. R. Colvin died in September, 1857.

GATES OF SOMNATH

These stand on the southern side of the Anguri Bagh, and form an interesting memento of the Afghan expedition of 1842. At that date they were the doors guarding the tomb of that scourge of India, Mahmud of Ghazni. As such the

British army believed them to be the still more famous gates of Somnath wrenched from the great Hindu temple in Guzarat, by Mahmud, in 1025. They were brought back as spoils of war, and paraded through northern India on a triumphal car. Finally, they were deposited in Agra. They are twelve feet high and nine feet wide. Like the originals they are beautifully and elaborately carved. Investigation, however, revealed them to be of Himalayan cedar bearing cufic inscriptions, whereas the Somnath doors were of sandal wood.

JAHANGIRI MAHAL

This great sandstone palace is frequently considered quite the finest and most significant building in the fort. Jahangir is said to have erected it as residence for his Hindu mother Mariam Zamani, and for his Hindu wife, Jodh Bai. The latter was mother to Jahan. Not content with loading it with an indescribable wealth of carving, Jahangir caused every square inch of walls and ceilings to be further adorned with brilliant colours and gold leaf. The fact that the architectural style is similar to that of Akbar's palaces at Fatehpur Sikri has led to the inference that it, too, dates from the greatest of the Moghuls. Against this other authorities point out that much of Akbar's adjoining palace was demolished to make room for it.

Originally the Jahangiri Mahal was a two-storeyed palace. It possessed seven courts, all of which were open to the sky, and corner towers, three-storeyed and octagonal, crowned with the usual kiosks. The great gate was in the centre of the western face. The dimensions of the site are given as 261 feet from north to south, and 288 feet from east to west. The east court is shaped like a capital T. From its inner angles, to north and south, stairways communicate with the roof, where stand various pavilions of red sandstone exquisitely, and intricately carved with bird and other designs. Here, too, are reservoirs whence water was supplied to the baths, tanks and fountains of the Khas Mahal and Anguri Bagh. Between these staircases runs the noted east vestibule, either extremity of which terminates in an arched hall. Behind lies the library famous for its gilding and colour decoration. To north is that portion of the palace subsequently appropriated by Shah Jahan. The octagonal tower pavilion appertaining thereto is described by Tavernier as covered with foliage of gold and azure. According to the French jeweller, it was Jahangir's intention to have it roofed with wrought silver. For this purpose he despatched messengers to the Portuguese settlement at Goa to obtain the necessary craftsmen. He further proposed to suspend clusters of grapes, formed of rubies and emeralds, from the ceiling of the verandah.

The central quadrangle is seventy-six feet square and is surrounded by two-storeyed facades of great beauty. The most elaborate of the courts is to south-west. Under British rule, a Military Prison stood to south of the Jahangiri Mahal. When the present King-Emperor, George V, visited Agra as Prince of Wales, in December, 1905, he requested its removal. This was subsequently effected.

HAUZ JAHANGIRI

Nicknamed Jahangir's bath this huge basin was found buried in front of the palace shortly after the mutiny. It is hewn out of a single block of porphyry, and is five feet high, eight feet in diameter and twenty-five feet in circumference. Steps are cut in the inner and outer sides. Traces are still visible of very fine carving. In addition a mutilated inscription records the name of Jahangir, and the date A.D. 1611. In that year the Emperor was married to the famous Nur Jahan, hence the supposition that it was a gift to her. Undoubtedly it was a cistern. Hindu tradition associates it with the five Pandu Princes, heroes of the Mahabharata, and founders of Indraprastha, the earliest Delhi. As such it is styled Bhima Raja-ka-kundi, or Bhima Raja's Bang bowl. Since it was dug up, it has experienced several changes of site. For many years it stood in Cantonment Gardens. From there it was brought back to the fort and placed in front of the Diwan-i-Am. Ultimately it was transferred to its present position in the courtyard near the Amar Singh Gate.

AKBARI MAHAL

The remains of this once extensive sandstone palace lie to south-east of the Jahangiri Mahal. Age blackened, neglected and dark they consist of gloomy courts surrounded by self-contained quarters. They have been identified as the southern section of the Great Moghul's seraglio described by de Laët as comprising three sets of apartments, into which the women were shut. As such each was named after the particular day of the week on which the Emperor visited it, hence one was styled Sunday, a second, Tuesday and the third, Saturday. De Laët writes: 'In addition, there is a fifth set of women's apartments, to which foreign women are brought up for the pleasure of the king. This is called the Bangali Mahal.' Akbar's Palace occupies the site of an infinitely older edifice, traces of which have been uncovered by excavation.

BAOLI AKBARI

Near to the Bangali Burj is a huge well ten feet in diameter. Steps lead down to the water. On the way they pass five tiers of halls. The well was worked by means of a drum affixed to a beam in an octagonal chamber. Originally these subterranean rooms were probably richly gilt, and painted and sumptuously fitted up as a hot weather retreat for the Emperor and his nobles. Here, on rich carpets and silken cushions, the Great Moghul would doubtless recline smoking, or drinking wine, a golden tray of fruit before him, prior to drifting into an opium enchanted dream. The big baoli is attributed to Akbar. It may be of still earlier date. In his memoirs, Baber records : 'There was an empty space within the fort of Agra between the palace and the ramparts. I directed a large well to be constructed on it twenty-four feet square. In the language of Hindustan, a big well with steps down into it is called a wain. The wain was begun before the garden was laid out. They were busy digging it during the rains, but it fell in several times smothering the workmen. After my holy war against Rana Sanka, I gave orders for finishing it, and a very excellent wain was completed. Inside was an edifice of three storeys. The lowest has three halls, and you descend to it by the well by means of stairs. Passages connect the three halls, each of which is higher than the other by three steps. In the lowest of all, when the waters subside, there is a flight that goes down to the well. In the middle storey, is a hall of carved stone and close by it is a dome for the oxen to turn in as they move the water wheel round. The uppermost tier consists of a single hall, from either side of which is a staircase. Straight opposite to the entrance is a stone engraved with the date of the building. By the side of the well, a shaft has been sunk to half its depth. Water is raised to it. A second wheel lifts the water to the level of the ramparts whence it flows into the upper gardens.'

SALIMGARH

Occupying the highest ground within the Fort is the fragment of a palace attributed to Sher Shah and his son Salim, the immediate predecessors of Akbar at Agra. This lies to west of the Diwan-i-Am outside the wall of the Great Court, and consists of a two-storeyed house, elaborately carved in the style associated with Akbar's buildings at Fatehpur Sikri. It faces the modern barracks and is said to have been the Naubhat Khana, or Music Hall where the Great Moghuls orchestra performed. Ferguson declares it equal in beauty to any specimen of decorative art in India.

AMAR SINGH DARWAZA

A descending ramp runs from the southern gate of the Diwan-i-Am to the Amar Singh Darwaza. This great portal dates from Akbar and bears the inscription 'Allahu Akbar Ala.' (God is great and omnipotent). Near it Amar Singh, Maharaja of Jodhpur, is said to have met his tragic death in 1644. It was by this gate that Lord Lake's victorious army entered the fort in 1803. The upper storey served as a lock-up for British Officers until the Military Prison was removed.

AFTERNOON

Visit the Taj Mahal and Roman Catholic Cemetery

TAJ MAHAL

Great love and passionate grief inspired the Crown of Palaces, the Taj Mahal. The foundations were laid deep in the heart of an Emperor for whom a suddenly darkened universe held but one ambition, one object in life, namely to build a tomb for his wife that should surpass anything the world had ever seen before or ever would again. That Shah Jahan succeeded in his heart's desire none can deny. The peerless white monument to his beloved consort Mumtaz-i-Mahal is the fairest shrine ever raised to love.

According to the Badshahnama Arjuna Banu, better known by her titles Mumtaz-i-Mahal, Exalted of the Palace, and Mumtaz-ul-Zamani, Wonder of the Age, was born in 1591. A Persian by descent she was daughter to the celebrated Prime Minister Asaf Khan, brother to the Empress Nur Jahan.

Her marriage to the Emperor Jahan occurred in 1612. She was twenty-one at the time. Although his second wife, Mumtaz-ul-Zamani enjoyed his undivided affection. She bore him eight sons and six daughters, but only six of their fourteen children survived infancy. The sharer of all his secrets she was the Emperor's confidential adviser and the inseparable companion of his travels. It was her bigoted prejudice against Christianity which inspired Jahan's hostile attitude towards Europeans during his father's life-time, and led him to open persecution of them as soon as he himself assumed imperial power. No doubt it was her early religious teaching, that made their son Aurangzib the fanatic he was.

As was her custom the Empress accompanied her husband on his campaign against Khan Jahan Lodi. At Burhanpur she gave birth to her fourteenth child, a princess styled Gauhara Begam, and died in camp on June 17, 1631, aged thirty-nine years and four months.

The grief distracted Emperor and his court assumed the white mourning of profound bereavement. It is further stated that his hair turned grey. The beloved body was temporarily buried at Burhanpur. Six months later, a vast funeral cortege accompanied it to Agra. Here it was laid in the garden of Man Singh, and a dome erected over it until such time as the Taj should be ready. Raja Man Singh, whose garden was thus signally honoured, was a Rajput General in the Imperial Army. He was nephew to Akbar's wife, Mariam Zamani, and brother-in-law to Jahangir, that Emperor having married his sister. While in Agra, Jahan visited the grave every Friday, when the fatiha, or prayers for the dead were repeated. On the anniversary of her death the Urs, or masses for the repose of her soul, were celebrated with considerable solemnity, at a cost of a lakh of rupees, half of which sum was distributed in alms.

ARCHITECT

Mystery enshrouds the name and nationality of the architect who designed the Taj. Manrique, a Spanish monk, who was at Agra in 1641, gives the credit to an Italian, Geronimo Verroneo, who died before the work was finished. Local accounts state that Ustad Isa was the chief architect, that Ismail Khan, a native of Turkey, built the dome, and that the inscriptions were made by Amanat Khan, a Persian from Shiraz. The marble inlay was probably the work of Austin de Bordeaux, a renegade French jeweller of genius, who is responsible for the mosaic decorations of Shah Jahan's palace at Delhi. He is known to have been at Agra, while the Taj was in course of construction. The *pietra dura* decorating the mausoleum is the finest in the world. The white marble used in the construction came from Jaipur, and the red sandstone from Fatehpur Sikri, while the world at large contributed towards the vast treasure of gold, silver, jewels, and semi-precious stones lavished upon the decorations.

The work was begun in 1631 and finished in 1648. Twenty thousand men are said to have been employed upon it daily. The mortality among them was frightful. Labour was forced. Grain rations were distributed by dishonest officials, who curtailed the allowance for their own benefit. Shah Jahan endowed the mausoleum with the revenues of thirty villages, said to yield a lakh annually. This sum was doubled by the rent of shops in the Jilan Khana, the great entrance court to south, and of the sarais in the adjacent town of Mumtazabad.

JILAN KHANA

The usual approach is by way of a handsome red sandstone gate house to west. This opens into a vast court with central porticoes in each face and arcaded cloisters around. Outside the western gate is a high platform to south of the road. Steps lead up to a dome crowned mausoleum, and dependent buildings. Here sleeps Satuinnisa Khanam, favourite lady-in-waiting to Mumtaz-i-Mahal, and sister of Jahangir's poet laureate, Talib Amli. She stayed watching by the grave of the Empress for six months at Burhanpur. Thereafter she accompanied the coffin to Agra. Highly accomplished, and a skilled linguist she was subsequently appointed governess to Shah Jahan's eldest, and favourite daughter, Jahanara Begam. The neighbouring mosque was erected in order that prayers might constantly be offered up for the repose of her soul.

The Outer Court, or Jilan Khana was completed about 1653. Its measurements are given as 412 feet north and south, by 971 feet east and west. Originally it served as a caravanserai and bazaar. The Badshahnama describes it as following: 'The area enclosed within the four walls is occupied by one hundred and twenty-eight rooms. . . . Near to the garden wall there are two Khawas-puras, one to east of the Jilan Khana, and the other to west, each being seventy-six yards by sixty-four yards, and containing thirty rooms with as many vestibules for attendants.'

SOUTH GATE

Through the Sirhi Darwaza, or Steps Gateway, a picturesque glimpse is caught of the old town of Mumtazabad, now the village of Tajganj, with its wide straight street, and overhanging balconies. Through the red arch drift the shrill voices of children intermingled with the deeper tones of men. Here the tomb attendants have dwelt since the death of the Empress. The site is of considerable interest. It is claimed to be that of Naumahta, once occupied by the houses and gardens of great nobles. Earlier still its walls enclosed the ancient city of Agra, which flourished centuries before Akbar. A spot is pointed out as the Kalandar, one of the gates of this forgotten capital. Shah Jahan renamed the town Mumtazabad, and rebuilt the portion of it entered from the Sirhi Darwaza. This was the Shahi, or Imperial Bazaar. It covered an area about 1,000 feet square crossed by two broad roads. In each of the four spaces thus formed stood a great caravanserai for those at work upon the Taj. As such it was an integral part of the mausoleum. Now the site is covered by Tajganj, whence the lakhouri bricks were extracted for restoring the Taj dalans. A house is shown as that occupied by the poet Nazir.

EAST GATE

The East Gate leads into Fathebad Road. Immediately outside it adjoins a high platform to south, dominated by yet another domed tomb. This shelters the remains of Sarhandi Begam, one of Shah Jahan's wives. Originally the white marble cenotaph was beautifully inlaid with semi-precious stones. The encircling terrace is vast and of unexpected charm and richness.

NORTH GATE

This is the main gate, a truly splendid entrance of red sandstone sumptuously inlaid with coloured mosaic on white marble, surmounted by kiosks, domes and glittering spires. The lofty octagonal hall is surrounded by rooms, one of which is utilized as a museum.

My first sight of the Taj was by moonlight. As I passed from the gloom of the massive portal into the silver radiance of the night I paused, spell-bound, at the top of the flight of steps leading down to the flower-scented garden. Before me stretched an avenue of cypress trees, straight, and black and melancholy, like mourners in a long procession. They followed a wide marble track that glimmered with a ghostly whiteness, while down the centre flowed a silent stream. In the distance a single star shone from out the inner darkness of a wondrous dome that rose, pure and white and strangely still, above a marble terrace, at the corners of which four tall minarets stood watching and waiting.

The warm night air was heavy with the perfumed breath of sleeping flowers. The single yellow light burnt steadily above the tomb of Mumtaz-i-Mahal. The white dome and sentinel towers emitted an unearthly radiance, while over all hung the moon, a magic lantern suspended from a sapphire sky. The atmosphere was one of all pervading melancholy. It was too sad and too beautiful for words. In that moment I realized 'the luxury of grief.'

From the main gate a stone causeway, divided down the middle by a water channel and bronze fountains, leads between a double row of cypress trees to the mausoleum. This stands on two terraces, the lower of red sandstone and the upper of white marble, 313 feet square, paved in a chessboard design with black and white marble. Each corner supports a three storeyed minaret.

The entrance is framed by an archway, sixty-six and a half feet high, inscribed, about the upper part, with Arabic texts, the big black lettering of which stands out boldy from the snowy whiteness of the facade. Beyond the beautiful portico a vestibule admits to the central chamber, octagonal in shape and surmounted by a lofty dome of curious echoes. The cenotaph of the Empress occupies the centre of the marble floor. Above it swings a beautiful bronze lamp, inlaid with gold and silver, from Egypt, the gift of Lord Curzon.

The tomb of the Emperor is slightly to one side and is raised some twelve inches above the other. Over each pious hands have scattered rose petals. The dying flowers fill the dim white hall with a sweet strange fragrance, and a suggestion of something unearthly.

Both graves are of white marble exquisitely and elaborately inlaid with mosaic in semi-precious stones. They are enclosed by an octagonal screen of white marble, pierced by two openings so wonderfully and delicately fretted as to suggest the finest lace. Gazing at it makes it almost seem as though a spider had been at work in marble. The indescribably lovely screen displays a flower border in coloured mosaic so minutely worked that no less than sixty-one tiny pieces of many shaded gems are united in one rose.

The present screen was substituted by Aurangzib Shah for one of wrought gold originally placed about the cenotaph of the Empress by Shah Jahan. On the anniversary of her wedding and on Friday nights a canopy, entirely composed of pearls, was spread over her tomb. This was carried off by the Sayyids Hussain Ali and his brother Abdalla, as were the diamonds, and other jewels of immense value, with which the tomb was studded.

In conformity with Muhammadan custom the real graves are in a crypt immediately under the central chamber containing the cenotaph. A steep passage leads down to this vault, where the sarcophagi are almost identical with those above. Although now plain to bareness the encircling walls and ceiling were once covered with sheets of purest gold, the same precious metal lining the grave wherein the Empress was laid to rest.

Dear as his wife was to him the Emperor had never intended to share her mausoleum. His idea was far more magnificent. But for the rebellion of his four sons, and his consequent dethronement and long captivitiy in the Jasmine Tower of the citadel at Agra, Jahan would have carried out his intention of erecting a still more majestic durgah for himself on the opposite bank of the Jumna. A white marble bridge, decorated in the same splendid style, would have connected the two. The idea did not appeal to Aurangzib. That austere Moslem laid his father beside his mother in the Taj Mahal, where, beneath their elaborate monuments of white marble and jewelled flowers, at a depth of six feet in the earth, lie the mortal remains of the Exalted of the Palace and her imperial lover.

JAMAT KHANA

This is the large mosque-like building to east of the Taj, whence it is separated by a spacious court. In the centre of the latter is a tank. Near by steps, enclosed by a railing, lead down to a number of basement apartments, evidently intended as a retreat in hot weather. Fourteen of these myterious rooms stretch along the river face of the great terrace. From the back of each a door connects with an inner lobby.

The court above has a curious design let into the pavement. This is a slate model of the gilt pinnacle of the Taj, and measures 30 feet 6½ inches from north to south. It is said to exactly duplicate the original.

The Jamat Khana, or Place of Assembly is a magnificent edifice, and was intended to accommodate the company gathered in honour of the Urs of the Empress. It would be almost impossible to excel the splendour of the interior decorations. Fortunately it is no longer let out to honeymoon couples, and others as a travellers bungalow. From the northern end the ruins of the once splendid palaces of nobles may be seen stretching along the banks of the river. The small two storeyed octagonal kiosk, on the further side of the Jumna, is believed to mark the site whereon Shah Jahan proposed to build his own mausoleum.

IMPERIAL MOSQUE

Very similar in design to the Jamat Khana, the Mosque is an even more magnificent building. It stretches along the western extremity of the great terrace and is similarly flanked by triple storeyed octagonal minars of red sandstone, with pierced stone window screens and balustrades, white marble domes and gilt pinnacles. The pavilion overhanging the river commands a romantic view of the garden residences lining the water's edge in Moghul times. Known as the Baisai Minar tradition asserts that one, or more houses occupied the site of the northern tower. These Jahan attempted to purchase. The inhabitants, however, presented him with the ground on condition that the edifice erected thereon should perpetuate their name.

The floor of the mosque is divided into 566 prayer spaces by lines of yellow black and white. The Mimbar, or pulpit, is of white marble and is mounted by three steps. The three Mihrabs, or recesses in the west wall, are also of white marble relieved with coloured zigzag inlay. Raised floral designs, adorn ceilings and walls under a coating of white stucco. The many red arches bear scroll borders in white marble. The Zenana chapel lies to north.

TEMPORARY TOMB

The Masjid overlooks a small red brick enclosure 16 feet by 19 feet. The walls are 6½ feet high but the roof is gone. This was the temporary tomb, where the embalmed body of the Empress lay for so many years. Flowering creepers, chiefly vivid purple bourgainvillier, and the rich yellow of Bignonia Venusta, spread a brightly coloured pall over the ruin.

THE ROMAN CATHOLIC CEMETERY

This ancient burial ground is one of the earliest Christian cemeteries in India. It dates from the beginning of the seventeenth century when the site was granted to the Portuguese missionaries by Akbar. The district is now known as Padri Tola, and includes the Roman Catholic Cathedral and the old Church.

Many quaint tombs are to be found in the cemetery, the most conspicuous of which are of Moghul design. A mausoleum of this kind is erected to the memory of that notorious Swiss soldier of fortune, Walter Reinhard.

He, it was, who married the wealthy Begam of Sardhana

in Meerut, and was commonly known as 'Sumroo,' a native corruption of the nickname 'Le Sombre' given to him by his comrades in the early days of his strange career. Under another red sandstone dome sleeps Enaet Mussy Bourbon, a descendant of the French Royal House. The most imposing monument is that of Colonel Hessing, an officer in the army of Maharaja Daulat Rao. He was Governor of Agra at the time of his death, and the big tomb was erected by his widow. In a humble grave in the grass lies Tieffenthaler, the great traveller. The Campo Santo also contains the tomb of Joseph de Castro best known to fame as executor to Verronio, the architect of the Taj, while in the mortuary chapel sleep those good Fathers Manuel Danhaya, '*morto pe lo fe*,' August 2nd, 1635, and Manuel Garcia 'died for the faith' on March 23rd, 1634. Both had been taken prisoners at the fall of Hughli, finally expiring in prison at Agra as the result of constantly refusing Shah Jahan's request to embrace the faith of Islam. Whatever their sufferings in life, in death they were not denied Christian burial.

SECOND-DAY—MORNING

Drive to Itmad-ud-Daulah's Tomb, Chini-Ka-Rauz and Ram Bagh.

TOMB OF ITMAD-UD-DAULAH

The famous tomb of Itmad-ud-Daulah lies on the left bank of the Jumna, and differs, in several respects, from the familiar domed structures common to Moghul sepulchral architecture. It is specially interesting for many reasons, chief among them being that Itmad-ud-Daulah was grandfather to Mumtaz-i-Mahal, the lady buried in the Taj.

Jahangir's Prime Minister possessed a history so uncommon as to deserve telling. When quite a young man he set out from Persia, accompanied by his wife and small children, to seek his fortunes in India. He had a relative at the court of the Great Moghul, and hoped that family influence would help him on. While crossing the desert of Scind provisions gave out, and he and his family were reduced to desperate straits. At this juncture his wife gave birth to a daughter. With starvation staring them in the face the unhappy parents decided to abandon the poor little thing. She was placed under a tree and left. As the distance between mother and child increased, the former's distress became more than she could bear. She implored her husband to return, at all costs, and fetch the baby. He did so. Great was his horror to see a huge snake approaching the tree. He was only just in time to save the infant. As he restored her to her mother's arms a caravan came in sight, and their troubles were at an end.

Once arrived at Akbar's court his exceptional talents soon won the Persian both position and honours. In addition to his name of Mirza Ghias-ud-Din he received the title of Itmad-ud-Daulah by which he is most usually known. Meanwhile the baby born in the desert grew into a beautiful and accomplished girl to whom her parents gave the musical name Mihr-un-Nissa. Fate or chance so willed that Prince Salim, the heir apparent, saw the girl and fell violently in love with her. For some reason Akbar refused to sanction the match. Instead he married her to Sher Afkhan, one of his Generals, and dispatched both to Bengal.

A ROYAL ROMANCE

Apparently neither time nor absence had the effect of quenching the Prince's passion. No sooner was his father dead, and he had mounted the masnad under the title Jahangir, than the new Emperor sent word to the General in Bengal commanding him to divorce his wife. This Sher Afkhan refused to do. The refusal was his death warrant.

During the second year of Jahangir's reign complaints, real or feigned, were brought to him regarding Sher Afkhan's conduct as Governor of Bardwan. The Emperor immediately appointed his foster brother, Sheikh Khubu, Viceroy of Bengal, with instructions to bring the offender to book. This the Viceroy proceeded to do. Sher Afkhan was summoned to his presence. A dispute followed whereupon Sher Afkhan ran Sheikh Khubu through the body. A minute later he, himself, fell pierced by a score of spears.

The widow and her little daughter were promptly conveyed to the Emperor's palace. There they were assigned apartments in the immediate vicinity of the Empress Dowager, Sultana Rukya Begam, a princess of the house of Taimur. Through some strange whim of the Emperor's, the woman who, as a girl, had inspired him with such passionate love, was given the poorest quarters in the harem, and only allowed a beggarly pittance with which to support herself, her child and few attendants. It is even asserted that Mihr-un-Nissa supplemented her insufficient income by doing fine needle work for the Begams.

During four years the beautiful and accomplished daughter of Itmad-ud-Daulah led this gloomy and restricted existence. At the end of that time she was summoned to a festival in honour of Nau Roz, New Year's Day. All unconsciously she attracted the Emperor's attention. Immediately his old infatuation returned with full force. Mihr-un-Nissa was then thirty-four years of age. A splendid marriage ceremony was arranged and, as Nur Mahal, or Light of the Palace, the newly made Empress maintained her coveted position as favourite wife until the Emperor's death on October 28, 1627. From that date she abandoned pomp and ceremony and, retiring into private life, wore the plain white dress of a Muhammadan widow until her demise nineteen years later.

Possibly no woman has ever enjoyed such absolute power as fell to the lot of Nur Jahan in her capacity of favourite wife to Jahangir. Naturally of an indolent and pleasure loving disposition, and much addicted to wine and opium, the Emperor was well content to hand the reigns of Government over to his energetic consort, whom, he declared, was capable of conducting all affairs.

Nur Jahan sat in the Emperor's place in the Jharokha, or imperial balcony, whence she conferred with the Ministers of State and generally transacted the business of the vast Moghul empire. Her name appeared on the gold coinage and on state documents. As was only natural she looked well after the fortunes of her family. Her father, and her no less able brother, Asaf Khan were advanced to the highest position in the imperial gift. She married her niece, the famous Mumtaz-i-Mahal, to Prince Khurram, afterwards Shah Jahan.

She, herself, had only one child, her daughter by her first husband, whom she married to Jahangir's youngest son, the handsome but ill-fated Prince Shahryar.

It was Nur Jahan Begam who built the splendid mausoleum on the left bank of the Jumna to her father, Itmad-ud-Daulah, and to her mother.

CHINI-KA-RAUZ

A little beyond the tomb of Itmad-ud-Daulah is a mausoleum known as Chini-ka-Rauz, said to be the last resting place of Afzal Khan, a Persian poet. As a matter of fact, Shukr-ullan-Khan was the man buried here. He was Prime Minister to Shah Jahan, and died at Lahore in 1639. His body was brought to Agra and interred in the tomb he had built for himsef, a red sandstone structure gaily decorated with brightly coloured tiling.

RAM BAGH

This was the first Moghul garden ever laid out in India. In his 'Memoirs' Baber gives the following account of it. 'In consequence of the want of beauty, and of the disagreeable aspect of the country, I gave up the intention of making a garden; but as no better spot presented itself near Agra I was finally compelled to make the best of this same spot. I first sank the large well that supplies the baths with water. I next fell to work on that piece of ground where the tamarind trees and the octagonal tank are. I then proceeded to construct the large tank and surrounding enclosure, and the tank and grand hall of audience in front of the stone palace. I proceeded to finish the garden of the private apartments, the apartments themselves and the baths. In this way, without neatness or order, Hindu fashion, I produced edifices and gardens possessed of considerable regularity. In every garden

I planted beds with roses and narcissi. The men of Hind, who had never before seen palaces so planned, or laid out with so much beauty, gave the name of Kabul to the bank of the Jumna where the palaces stand.'

Upon his death in 1530 the body of Baber lay for six months in Ram Bagh prior to its removal to Kabul for burial. The Garden of Ease was a favourite resert of the Empress Nur Jahan. Two houses, on the stone terrace overhanging the river, possess a number of subterranean chambers from which the ladies of the harem are said to have fished. The houses are now used as Dak bungalows.

AFTERNOON

Drive out to Sikandarah

THE IDGAH

This is a large walled enclosure on the northern side of Ajmir Road. Tradition asserts it to have been built by Jahan in forty days. High embattlemented walls surround a court measuring about 570 feet by 830 feet. Towers marked each of the four corners. The Idgah proper stands on the western end on the usual raised platform. It is a species of red sandstone mosque of seven arches 159 feet long and forty feet deep, where the Emperor annually celebrated the feast of Id-ul-Fitr. This follows the long fast of Ramazan as the Christian Easter succeeds Lent.

SIKANDARAH

This village derives its name from Sultan Sikandar Lodi the first sovereign to make his capital at Agra. It is even supposed that the present village occupies the site of his city, a surmise confirmed by the scattered traces of buildings, which point to the place once having been of considerable size and importance. To-day the only surviving structure of the vanished capital is known as the Baradari of Sikandar Lodi. It dates from 1495, and consists of a two storeyed red stone edifice. Square in plan, each side extends 142 feet while a carved octagonal tower rises from each of the four corners.

In 1623, Jahangir converted the palace of the former Afghan monarch into a mausoleum for his mother, Mariam-ul-Zamani, the Rajput wife of Akbar, and sister to Raja

Bhagwan Dass of Ambar, the ancient Jaipur. Her cenotaph stands in the centre of the upper storey. The actual grave consists of a simple white slab placed in the middle vault of the fifty underground apartments, wherewith the foundations are honeycombed.

THE HORSE

Sikandarah lies five miles from Agra and can be reached by either of two roads. The older is not so direct, but is the more interesting. It passes a number of half ruined mausolea. On the left side, hidden by the railway line, but quite easy of access, is a curious life-sized figure of a horse in red sandstone and a small tomb. According to tradition the favourite horse and sais of a wealthy nobleman were killed on this spot. He buried them here and caused the monuments to be erected over their remains.

Across the fields, on the opposite side of the road, are the mausolea of Sahabat Khan, Chief Treasurer to Shah Jahan, and of Sadiq Khan, sometime spiritual guide to Akbar.

AKBAR'S TOMB

Sikandarah is now chiefly interesting as the burial place of Akbar. His unique mausoleum has no parallel among Persian or other Saracenic monuments, architects agreeing that the design was evolved from that of a Buddhist vihara. The site was selected by the Great Moghul, who chose the Garden of Bihishtabad, near the old Lodi Palace, now the tomb of his wife. At his death, little more than the garden walls and a few preliminary preparations had been accomplished. For some cause or other the work proceeded very slowly although three thousand labourers were employed upon it.

In his peculiarly candid memoirs, Jahangir tells how, in the third year of his reign, he made a pilgrimage on foot to his father's tomb. He was so dissatisfied with what he saw that he caused the greater part to be demolished and entirely reconstructed at a cost of fifteen lakhs of rupees. The mausoleum was finally finished in 1613, eight years after Akbar had passed to rest.

The Garden of Bihishtabad is 150 acres in extent and is enclosed by a battlemented wall twenty-four feet high. This last was built in two stages. The original wall, as approved by Akbar, reached up twelve feet nine inches. It was raised to its present elevation by Jahangir in order that the grounds might not be overlooked by passers on elephants and camels. The four corners are emphasised by octagonal bastions of picturesque aspect, forty-three feet high. All are crowned by octagonal kiosks finished off with domes, excepting the one in the north-west angle.

Four splendid sandstone gateways command the enclosure, one in the middle of each wall. That, on the west side, was used as a Masjid.

The main entrance is to the south. It is the largest and is square in plan the corners dominated by white marble minarets of circular shape. Marble mosaic completely covers the exterior, while the interior is divided up among a number of apartments, one of which, a big arched chamber above the portico, was known as the Naubat Khana, or music gallery. From here kettle drums were beaten, in honour of the dead, at dawn and again one watch after sunrise.

The great portal owes much of its effect to a central arch, 70 feet high, profusely inlaid with marble in the style destined to become characteristic of later Moghul architecture.

A broad causeway leads from each of the four entrances to the mausoleum, a strikingly beautiful and solemn edifice of pyramidal form, each of the five graduated storeys encircled by arcaded cloisters. Those surrounding the lowest floor are so vast that a regiment of British dragoons, quartered there-by Lord Lake early in the nineteenth century, hardly occupied any appreciable space.

The base of the mausoleum is a square, each side of which measures 339 feet. It rests upon a raised terrace 496 feet 3 inches by 496 feet 10 inches. With its arabesque tracery, Hindu carving and Buddhist form the curious and beautiful building bears witness to the composite faith of the Great Moghul who sleeps therein.

The tomb is entered from the south by an arched porch, decorated with marble mosaic, from either side of which a staircase runs up to a marble pavilion three flights above. Similar porticoes and staircases characterize the north, east and west doors. A splendid vestibule of cruciform shape, admits to a dark, inclined passage, 105 feet long and 6 feet wide, that gives access to the sepulchre. This consists of a domed vault, 38 feet square, dimly lit by four small window openings. It is stone paved and the walls are decorated in royal blue and gold, in effective contrast to the simple white marble sarcophagus. Formerly rich rugs were spread upon the floor while the books, clothing and armour of the Emperor lay beside his grave. These were carried off to Bharatpur by the Jats, and it is not known what became of them.

Returning to the ground floor this is partitioned off by handsomely chiselled screens of white marble, and contains a number of graves. East of the south vestibule are two interesting tombs. The larger is sacred to the lovely Aram Begam, a daughter of Akbar, and the favourite sister of Jahangir.

THE CENOTAPH

Marble trellis work of rare beauty and intricacy of design surrounds the topmost storey of the mausoleum. Open to the sky the fifth and last floor is encircled by a white marble cloister divided into forty bays by slender piers of cruciform shape, from which spring graceful arches.

The floor is of tessellated marble. In the centre stands a marble platform the sides panelled in a chessboard design with black white and mottled buff and grey marble ; the last variety being peculiar to Jaisalmer. This supports the cenotaph hewn out of a solid block of white marble, and measuring 6 feet 10 inches long by 2 feet 7 inches wide, and 3 feet 3 inches high.

At the head and foot delicately beautiful floral ornamentation forms a frame about the inscriptions 'Allahu Akbar,' 'God is Great,' and 'Jalla Jalahuhu,' 'Glorified be His glory.' Round the two sides and on the top the ninety-nine titles of the Creator are carved in *alto relievo*, bordered with the finest chiselling of flowers and plants, amid which appear the dahlia, almond blossom and lily. The upper part is further decorated with the Kalam Dan, or pen box usual to the graves of Moslem men, those of their women displaying a writing tablet as distinctive sign of femininity.

THE KOH-I-NUR

At the northern end, or head of the cenotaph, is an elaborately carved pedestal, 2 feet 9 inches high, composed of two blocks of marble. This was once covered in gilding and, according to tradition, supported the famous diamond known as the Koh-i-Nur. Be that as it may there is no doubt but that its original purpose was to hold the chiragh, or lamp which, in conformity with Muhammadan custom, is lit at night over a tomb to mark the sanctity of the spot.

It was an ancient Hindu custom to honour Kings, and other distinguished guests by placing a diamond, or similar glittering precious stone in a lamp in place of either wick or ghi. Kalhana alludes to this practice in the Rajatarangini, or River of Kings. Very possibly it appealed to Akbar who may have commanded that it should be observed in the case of his tomb. The curious and bizarre attracted him powerfully.

Although now open to the sky the unfinished mausoleum was designed to have a dome. When Finch visited Sikandarah in 1611 he described the cenotaph as covered by a rich tent. He adds that it was to be roofed over by a dome of 'most curious white and speckled marble, the ceiling to be of pure sheet gold, richly inwrought.'

KANCH MAHAL

A dak bungalow stands in the mausoleum grounds. There tea and other refreshments may be procured. A little beyond is the Kanch Mahal, a two storied building of red sandstone. It is much carved, and displays encaustic tiling and bay windows. The upper floor is reached by a staircase from outside. Built by Jahangir as a country house for his wife, Jodh Bai, it is considered an admirable specimen of seventeenth century domestic architecture. A short distance further on is a second building, somewhat similar in construction, known as the Suraj Bhan-ka-Bagh.

THIRD-DAY

FATEHPUR SIKRI

Fatehpur-Sikri, or City of Victory, lies twenty-three miles south-west of Agra. It is approached by an excellent metalled road planted with trees, which leads through the villages of Midhakur and Kiraoli. Quaint milestones, some 20 feet high are encountered at intervals. These date from the days of Babar, and are known as kosminars, a kos measuring about two miles. A new railway runs out to Fatehpur-Sikri, at which place a very fine dak bungalow has recently been erected at a cost of Rs. 75,000.

Fatehpur Sikri stands on the site occupied by Babar's camp during the famous battle between the Moghul forces and the Rajputs of Chitor, in 1527. When the fortunes of the day hung in the balance the Emperor made a vow to renounce wine if victory were vouchsafed him. Some authorities say the city owes its name to this decisive success of Babar's, but the majority agree that it was called the City of Victory by Akbar after his triumphs in Gujarat. It enjoys the unique distinction among towns of being entirely the work of one man.

THE SAINT

In ancient times a village called Sikri stood on the spot destined to become for a brief space the capital of a great Empire. It was the home of stone-cutters who worked in the neighbouring sandstone quarries. The place was of no importance until a noted Mussulman saint, Sheik Salim Chishti took up his abode there in a cave. This celebrated recluse, the most noted Pir, or Saint, of his age in Hindustan, came of a family renowned for religion and good works, being a descendant of the far-famed Sheikh Farida-i-Shakarganj. He took the name of Chishti in honour of his spiritual father, a holy man from Chisht, in Persia. The austerities he practised, together with the fame of his sanctity, and miraculous powers soon reached Agra and were told to the Emperor. Akbar was then childless, none of his children having survived infancy. On his way back from a campaign against the revolted Uzbek nobles Akbar accordingly halted at Sikri, to pay his respects to the Sheikh and request his prayers on behalf of a son and heir.

Various tales are told of the interviews between the ascetic and the Emperor. One account describes how Akbar was twice dismissed with unsatisfactory replies. On the third occasion Salim Chishti's little son cried out, 'Father, why do you send the Conqueror of the World away in despair?' 'Because,' said the holy man, 'no son is destined for him unless somebody will give the life of a child.' 'I will' exclaimed the boy and forthwith expired.

This legend probably originated in an attempt to explain the intense superstitious awe in which Salim Chishti was held by the Emperor.

As a matter of fact versus fiction, the Sheikh advised Akbar to send his Hindu wife, Mariam-ul-Zamani, to reside at Sikri. Akbar followed this counsel and the Empress took up her abode in the household of the saint. Here a son was born to Akbar within the year. The little prince was named Salim, after the Sheikh but later adopted the title Jahangir on becoming Emperor.

In gratitude for the divine favour accorded to him Akbar determined to erect a city and make his capital in the place where his prayers had met with such ready response.

As was only natural Salim Chishti was henceforward a

persona grata at Court. His family enjoyed many exclusive privileges both under Akbar and his immediate successors. For instance the Sheikh's grandson Byazzid, whose mother had nursed the heir apparent on the day that he was born, was, on Jahangir's accession promoted to a Mansab of three thousand with the title Mir Azzam Khan. At his death he was buried at Fatehpur Sikri.

Another daughter of the saint acted as foster mother to the prince. Her son Sheikh Khubu was his foster brother. Many years later, when, as Emperor, Jahangir coveted Mihr-un-Nissa, the beautiful wife of Sher Afkhan, he despatched his foster brother against that general. In the tragedy which ensued both Sheikh Khubu and Sher Afkhan lost their lives, but the Emperor gained his heart's desire, and Mihr-un-Nissa became the famous Empress Nur Jahan.

THE DESERTED CITY

Towards the latter part of his long reign political reasons caused Akbar to abandon Fatehpur Sikri and to re-establish his headquarters at Agra. The departure of the Emperor and his Court led to the evacuation of the town. Soon the once splendid city became a resort of wild beasts and dangerous characters, who took up their abode amid the deserted palaces and great gateways. From then on Fatehpur Sikri appears to have played little, or no part in history, until the autumn of 1719, when it again enjoyed a brief spell of imperial favour. In that year Muhammad Shah — the Emperor placed upon the peacock throne by those king-making Sayyids, Hussain Ali and his brother Abdalla—held his first Darbar there on September 14th. The Court made but a short stay. Soon palaces and towers relapsed into silence. Nothing disturbs the stillness but the occasional screech of a peacock by day, or the hoot of an owl by night. These, with the bat and 'fretful porcupine' hold undisputed sway in the city hallowed by memories of the great Akbar.

The deserted capital is six miles in circumference. On three sides it is enclosed by high battlemented walls pierced by seven massive gateways. The fourth side was open, relying only for protection upon a large artificial lake constructed by Akbar. This has been drained off within the last few years as it rendered the district too unhealthy.

The Agra Gate, by which visitors usually enter, may be taken as typical of the other six. Abutting on to it is a spacious quadrangle surrounded by ruined cloisters. Troops were presumably quartered here.

Immediately inside the gate two roads meet. One leads through the modern town, and runs south west of the ruined capital to the Tehra Gate some two miles distant. The other is the highway to the palaces situated on the crest of the red sandstone ridge. This road was originally lined with small houses forming the bazaar. The greater part of the space enclosed within the city walls is littered with the stone remains of noblemen's mansions, baradaris, pavilions, and lesser dwellings. Mixed up with them are the houses constituting the modern town, where good daris and glass churis are manufactured.

NAUBAT KHANA

The first stopping place is the Naubat Khana. This is built in the form of a square, with four gateways, one on each side, which give admittance to a courtyard surrounded by low chambers. Here troops were quartered. From here, too, musicians announced the arrival and departure of the Emperor and played during state functions.

THE MINT

The road continues up the hill to the Taksal or Mint, a large quadrangular building, where gold and silver coins were first struck in 1577.

The chief officer of the mint was known as the Darogah. His staff consisted of the Sairafi, or assayer, the foreman, clerk, bullion buyer, treasurer, weigher, melter, plate maker, Zarrab, or flan-cutter, and the Sikkachi or puncher.

The metal was brought to the mint in small bars and distributed among a number of persons seated on the ground. These were provided with scales, hammers, a tool which combined the functions of chisel and punch, and large stones by way of anvils. The bars were cut up by guess work. If found too heavy, when weighed, a piece was clipped off, if too light a fragment was punched in to make up the deficiency.

The second process consisted of hammering the pieces into a round shape, about seven-eighths of an inch in diameter and one-eighth thick. They were then carried to the Sikkachi who placed each on a die fixed into the ground, between a second die he held in his right hand. His assistant next dealt a sharp blow with his mall and the impression was made. With this the coin was sent to the Treasury, ready for currency throughout the realm.

THE TREASURY

Almost a complete ruin the Treasury stands on the opposite side of the road. It consists of a quadrangle measuring 62 feet by 66½ feet. Rooms still enclose it to the east and south, those to the north and west having long since disappeared.

DIWAN-I-AM

The road next passes into the vast courtyard of the Diwan-i-Am, or Hall of Public Audience. In common with nearly all the buildings of Fatehpur Sikri it is entirely composed of red sandstone drawn from the neighbouring quarries. Its dimensions are 365 feet 5 inches from north to south, and 181 feet from east to west. Cloisters run round three sides, the western face being reserved for the Diwan-i-Am. This consists of a raised pavilion 23½ feet by 15 feet, protected by a ten feet wide verandah. In the centre is the elevated recess in the wall, or balcony which formed the Emperor's Judgment Seat. The cloisters were capable of seating thousands of litigants, suitors and others, who appeared before the Great Moghul to claim redress. The sunken roof above the Judgment Seat, with its walls carried up a height of 6 feet, provided a promenade for the ladies of the harem.

MAHAL-I-KHAS

Beyond the great quadrangle of the Diwan-i-Am is a second large courtyard measuring 326 feet by 210 feet. To west of this rises the important block of buildings known as the Mahal-i-Khas. Believed by some to have been the first of the palatial group erected by Akbar in the vicinity, the Mahal-i-Khas extends along a frontage of 559 feet and is 272 feet deep. It is divided into three main portions. The first contains Akbar's private apartment, the Khwabgah, or House of Dreams. In front lies a large hauza or tank, 95½ feet square, originally supplied with water from the elaborate works near the Elephant Gate. The centre of the tank displays a square platform whence radiate four stone causeways. To north-east is the Turkish Sultana's House, the Girls' School being to north-west. All three, namely, the Sultana's House, Khwabgah and Girls' School, are connected by a colonnade. This cut them off from the Pachisi Court, the second of the main portions into which the Mahal-i-Khas is divided. The third section comprises the Diwan-i-Khas, better known to fame as the Ibadat Khana, the Ankh Michauli and the Astrologer's Seat.

DIWAN-I-KHAS

Considered the most curious of the buildings at Fatehpur Sikri—no two of which are alike—the Diwan-i-Khas, or Hall of Private Audience is a red sandstone edifice of unique interior arrangement. Built by Akbar in 1575 it is the celebrated Ibadat Khana, where men of learning, and opposing religions assembled for debate on Friday nights. Listening to their arguments the Emperor evolved the idea of promulgating a new faith of his own, drawn from what he considered best in existing creeds, entitled the Divine Monotheism.

From outside the Diwan-i-Khas appears double storeyed. On entering it is found to consist of a single lofty chamber occupied by a massive octagonal column. This reaches to the sills of the upper windows, and is surmounted by an enormous capital formed of three tiers of radiating brackets curiously and wonderfully carved in Hindu style, the chiselling on the shaft or base being of a Saracenic character. The top of the pillar is arranged as a platform enclosed by pierced screens, similar screens characterizing the four broad passages which branch out to each angle of the building, connecting the summit of the column with the encircling gallery.

According to tradition Akbar's throne occupied the centre of this peculiarly isolated elevation. At the further extremities of the gangways were posted the four principal ministers of state, portfolio in hand. Suppliants stood on the floor below and were interrogated by the Emperor who, as the need arose, conferred with one, or other of his ministers. During the famous Friday night conferences those participating in the debates were assigned places in the round gallery, above which recesses may be seen, cut in the walls, at the north-west and south-east corners. These were cupboards for the storing of documents and other valuables. Each was secured inside by a slab of stone, and outside by a stone door fastened with a heavy padlock.

It is said that the unique plan of the Diwan-i-Khas was inspired by the Emperor's fear of assassination.

Four corner kiosks adorn the flat roof which is reached by two staircases hewn in the thickness of the walls.

PACHISI COURT

This is a paved court, to north of which stands the Diwan-i-Khas. It is laid out in black and white squares for the game of pachisi. The Emperor and his opponent sat upon the raised seat in the middle, beneath a fringed canopy of rich embroidered silk. Gaily attired slave girls acted as chess men, moving from square to square as directed.

ASTROLOGER'S SEAT

The north-west corner of the Pachisi Court is marked by a small Chattri, or covered platform of square shape, each side measuring 9 feet 9 inches. It is distinguished by the elaborate struts that support the flat roof, while the raised floor appears to have originally been enclosed by a stone railing. The style is that usual to Jaina architecture of the eleventh century. Known as the astrologer's seat it was the abode of a Yogi. In common with many great men Akbar was strongly attracted by the supernatural. He was a generous patron to soothsayers, and it is said that, in his desire to penetrate into the hidden mysteries of the past and future, he spent many hours after dark in deep and secret converse with the Brahmin in the Astrologer's Seat.

Abul Fazl tells how greatly the Emperor favoured this

class of Hindus. He granted them private interviews at night, questioning them concerning their articles of faith, occupations and supposed power of absenting the spirit from the body, as well as regarding alchemy, physiognomy and other occult arts. Once a year, on a night known as Sivrat, Akbar presided over a great meeting of all the jogis in the empire.

ANKH MICHAULI OR HIDE AND SEEK HOUSE

A few steps to west of the Diwan-i-Khas is a three roomed house built over extensive vaults. Called the Ankh Michauli it is reputed to have been the place where the ladies and children of the Court played hide-and-seek, a game in which Akbar often deigned to join them. Popular as this form of amusement was, it is extremely improbable that it was ever played in this particular building, as it stands outside the harem limits.

Far easier of credence is the suggestion that the Ankh Michauli was used as a bank, or repository for state papers and treasure. Entrance is from the east side where two staircases lead to the roof. In the upper part of the walls are deep recesses, or closets, originally provided with sliding stone slabs and padlocks similar to those in the Diwan-i-Khas. On the north and the west sides of the houses is a declivity surmounted by a double storeyed stone gallery, while at the north-west corner a steep staircase connects with the roadway below.

KHWABGARH

The southern façade of the Mahal-i-Khas consists of a range of buildings surmounted by the Khwabgarh, or House of Dreams, a small chamber used by Akbar as his sleeping apartment. Corridors connected it with the Turkish Sultana's

House, the Panch Mahal, Maryam's Kothi, and the Palace of Jodh Bai.

The main building is one storeyed, the skyline only broken by the imperial bedroom. The apartment to east had its walls covered with paintings, principally of flowers, traces still showing of poppies, peonies, tulips, roses and almond blossom. It was also provided with recesses for storing valuables, and had three entrances. Behind is a chamber 20 feet 9 inches wide by 42 feet 7 inches long, said to have been assigned to a learned Brahmin attached to the Court.

A blocked up doorway, in the western wall, led to the courtyard in front of the Record House. This was the approach by which courtiers entered and passed along a screened off passage to the Emperor's sleeping apartment above.

Surrounded by a verandah 9 feet 6 inches wide, Akbar's *sanctum sanctorem* testifies to his love of colour decoration. The walls were completely covered with paintings interspersed with Persian inscriptions written in gold on a chocolate ground, and bordered with fantastic designs in vermilion and azure, varied by edgings of royal blue and gold.

Cupboards consisted of oblong recesses 11½ inches deep sunk into the upper part of the walls. The interiors were painted sky blue, and the openings were filled in with stone lattice work.

GIRLS' SCHOOL

This is a low, unpretentious building situated in the north-west angle of the Mahal-i-Khas. It contains two rooms and has a verandah on its north-side.

TURKISH SULTANA'S HOUSE

In close proximity to the Girls' School, at the north-east corner of the Mahal-i-Khas, is the house of the Turkish

Sultana, a single chamber encircled by a verandah. Although so small, the building is the most beautiful in Fatehpur Sikri. Entirely composed of red sandstone, every inch of both exterior and interior is exquisitely carved, the facades being unrivalled in India for elaboration of detail. The roof is chiselled in imitation of old Italian tiling, while inside are depicted jungle scenes, flowers and birds.

Additional rooms were secured by dividing the verandah up into partitions, by means of stone screens.

On the west side is a portico 8 feet 8 inches wide, and 16 feet 4 inches long. Running the length of the top is a beautifully carved drip stone. A spacious verandah projects from the south-west corner, and, continuing northwards, unites with a cloister connecting with the Girls' School.

From the east verandah, stairs lead to a Turkish bath, at the south end of the Diwan-i-Am.

TURKISH BATH

The hammam, or bath accredited to the Turkish wife of Akbar, was separated from her house by a small garden which stretched as far as the wall of the Diwan-i-Khas, and was divided from the Pachisi Court by a stone wall. Steps at the southern end led to the roof of the Diwan-i-Am expressly screened by high fretwork, behind which the Begam and her ladies could promenade at will without being observed.

The exterior of the hammam is severely plain. Inside, however, the austerity of the building is enlivened by plaster and coloured designs. Close by is a stone tank, below which is another set of baths—those used by the Emperor. Water was obtained from a huge well sunk in solid rock and surrounded by tiers of domed chambers and galleries.

DAFTAH KHANA

Facing the Khwabgah, or house of Dreams, on the southern side of the courtyard, stands the Daftar Khana, or Record Chamber. This was Akbar's kutcheri, or office where he was in the habit of remaining late into the night listening to statements regarding affairs in various parts of the empire, giving orders and personally looking into accounts.

THE HOSPITAL

A wall separates the first collection of buildings, included under the comprehensive title Mahal-i-Khas, from the second great group comprised of Maryam's House, the Panch Mahal, Hospital, etc. The dividing wall is pierced by several doorways. One, near the Ankh Michauli, leads to the hospital, a low, single storeyed building chiefly interesting because of the evidence it affords that such institutions did exist in Hindustan, in the sixteenth century. The gabled roof is carved in the same manner as that over the Turkish Sultana's House, and represents tiling, the big stone blocks, from which it is constructed, being chiselled underneath into a most exquisite panelled ceiling.

The interior walls were coated with plaster, the doorways and windows displaying ornamental borders brightly painted in red and white. Stone partitions divided the twelve wards, small apartments measuring 14 feet by 9 feet 6 inches. These were provided with stone clothes pegs in the shape of animals' heads, let into the walls. The south side displayed a roomy verandah some 11 feet wide.

PANCH MAHAL

This extraordinary building occupies the centre of the imperial palaces to west of the Mahal-i-Khas. As its name implies, it is five-storeyed. Planned on the lines of a Buddhist vihara, each successive storey contracts until the topmost is merely a diminutive kiosk supported by four pillars.

The ground floor measures 72 feet 4 inches by 57 feet 11 inches and contains eighty-four sculptured columns, no two of which are alike. The second floor has fifty-six columns, the third, twenty, the fourth, twelve, and the fifth only four. Each storey is protected by an ornamental parapet, while the first was originally divided up into various apartments by means of perforated stone screens, the designs resplendent in gilt and vivid colours. Outer walls of stone fretwork insured privacy while allowing free passage to any passing breeze.

Here Akbar would repair in the evening accompanied by a few favoured friends. It is probable that the building was also used by the ladies of the harem.

MARYAM'S HOUSE

Originally entitled the Sonahra Makam, or Golden House, because of the gilding lavished upon its exterior and interior walls, this building stands in the enclosure immediately south of the Panch Mahal. Now known as Maryam's Kothi, it was the residence of Maryam-ul-Zamani, Akbar's third wife, sister to Raja Bhagwan Dass, and the mother of Jahangir Shah.

The house stands on a raised platform, and is of oblong shape measuring 59 feet 10 inches by 48 feet 5 inches. Three sides are encircled by a verandah, and the ground floor is divided up into four apartments. One of these is a long room extending from north to south. The other three are at right angles to it at the southern end. Upstairs are three more rooms. Steps lead on to the flat roof, where a pavilion marks the northern portion.

In common with all Akbar's buildings at Fatehpur Sikri, Maryam's Kothi is profusely carved. In this case, the subjects depicted are markedly Hindu, and, out of compliment no doubt to the Empress' solar descent, portray incidents in the life of Rama. In addition to its elaborate work the dwelling was further decorated with brilliantly coloured frescoes.

Referring to Akbar's love of painting Abul Fazl comments, 'The mixing of colour has been greatly improved. Most excellent painters are now to be found, Hindus, in particular, excelling in the art.'

MARYAM'S GARDEN

Adjoining the Sonahra Makam is an open area, once Queen Maryam's garden. Formerly enclosed by rubble walls faced with cement it was entered through a gateway flanked by a guard-house. The ground space was completely filled in with a stone pavement. The main water course ran from south to north, smaller channels dividing up the pleasance into squares lined with flowers, plants and shrubs arranged, Hindu fashion, in pots. The chief glory of the garden was the fish tank sheltered by a pretty little chattri, or pavilion. Steps led down to the water's edge on two sides. On the third, to north, are cusped niches, which, on festivals, were filled with coloured lamps. The outfall is carved to represent the scales of fishes.

To north of the tank was a second garden, 62 feet 8 inches by 92 feet 8 inches screened by a high wall.

MARYAM'S BATH

At the south-east corner of her garden is Queen Maryam's Bath, a square building with open sides measuring 26 feet each way, and 12 feet 6 inches high. Screens were fitted into the walls, while steps were cut at each corner of the tank for those who did not care to plunge in from the bank.

Water was supplied from the works near the Hiram Minar, portions of the conduit being still extant.

The now open garden was once jealously guarded by high walls, the penalty of passing which was death in its most terrible form to any but the duly authorized.

JODH BAI'S PALACE

Such is the name given to the large palace situated south-west of Maryam's House. Just why it is called after Jahangir's wife, Jodh Bai is problematical. The chief of Akbar's wives, the Badshah Begam, was entitled Sultana Rukujal. It is possible that the palace was hers, but hardly probable for she was a Muhammadan and the carvings everywhere are pronouncedly Hindu. The most feasible suggestion is that the greater portion of the zenana was lodged therein.

Sometimes alluded to as the Jahangiri Mahal the palace is the biggest building in Fatehpur Sikri. It is also supposed to be the first to have been erected there by Akbar. The bell and chain, one of the oldest forms of Hindu ornament, is freely cut on the stone piers. Colour decoration was lavished on the parapets, while the vivid turquoise encaustic tiling, on the wagon shaped roofs, is further quoted as proving the early date of the work.

The building possesses a peculiar interest in that it is self-contained and furnishes a unique example of a Muhammadan palace in the sixteenth century. It consists of a rectangular block, 231 feet 8 inches from north to south, and 215 feet from east to west, built around an open quadrangle measuring 179 feet by 161 feet 9 inches. The façades are unbroken by windows, or door openings, the only relief being a string course and embattlemented parapet. Domed kiosks appear at the north-west and south-east corners. Adjoining the northern end is the Hawa Mahal, or Wind Palace, and on the south are the private baths.

Roughly speaking the plan of Jodh Bai's Palace consists of four main double storeyed blocks, one in the centre of each side, connected by suites of rooms, or partitioned corridors, running along the ground level. The roofs are flat excepting over the central blocks to north and south, where they are gabled and overlaid by brilliant turquoise encaustic tiling.

There is only one entrance to the palace. It is through the main block on the east, which is arranged as a vestibule, above which are two small rooms with balconies. Tradition points to the central block on the west, as having been a chapel. Above it is a long room with a row of columns down the middle. Wagon shaped roofs of brightest blue distinguish the blocks to north and south. The intermediate floor, on the northern side, was used by Akbar as his dining room.

HAWA MAHAL

From the Emperor's dining room a doorway leads into the Hawa Mahal, or Air Palace, a large apartment enclosed by pierced sandstone screens. This was a favourite resort in warm weather and commands a delightful view. On the western side a staircase connected with the viaduct leading down to the Hathi Pol, or Elephant Gate.

All the roofs were utilized as promenades. Screened walks were obtained for the zenana by carrying the outer walls of the corridors a considerable height above the flat roof.

ZENANA BATHS

These lie immediately outside the south wall of the palace. They were reached by narrow passages, one to east and the other to west, of the southern main block. Situated between two yards enclosed by corridors the private baths occupy an area of 121 feet by 35 feet. The various apartments are dome crowned, and, like Turkish baths, were heated by hot air, the interior decoration consisting of gaily coloured plaster dados.

The zenana was well guarded. Inside it was watched over by women attendants described by Abul Fazl as 'active and sober.' Outside the inclosure a large number of trusty eunuchs kept watch and ward. Beyond again, at a proper distance, was a guard of faithful Rajputs, and finally there were the sentinels and porters of the gates.

A covered way, now destroyed, connected the palace with the Khwabgah, Akbar's sleeping apartment, in the House of Dreams.

STABLES

Behind the palace, and abutting on to its western wall are the Camel Stables 219 feet 8 inches long by 25 feet deep. The roof is flat and is supported by rows of perfectly plain stone pillars, which divide the interior into seventeen bays in length by three in width. A little beyond, are other stables with acommodation for 110 horses. Oblong in shape, these extend 298 feet 4 inches by 124 feet 6 inches, and enclose an open court measuring 278 feet by 80 feet. Each animal was attached by head ropes fastened to stone rings at either side of the manger, and again by heel ropes passed through stone posts fronting the long stone boxes.

BIRBAL'S HOUSE

A Brahmin by caste, and a Bhat, or minstrel by profession, Raja Birbal was one of the most noted figures in the coterie immediately encircling the Emperor. His name was originally Mahesh Das. Poor, but clear headed, he left Kalpi to further his fortunes at Court. There his witty sayings, coupled with his gift of Hindu verse soon raised him high in the imperial favour. He was awarded the dignity of Kab Rai, or Poet Laureate. Later on, he was given the title of Raja Bir Bal, with Nagarkot as Jagir. The next step elevated him to the coveted post of Prime Minister.

Not content with reposing his entire confidence in the Poet Laureate, Akbar admitted him to his close personal friendship. As favourite of the Emperor Raja Birbal was entrusted with many important missions. Finally, he was killed in battle, together with eight thousand of the Imperial troops, in the severest reverse Akbar's army ever suffered.

On learning of his favourite's death, Akbar went into public mourning, refusing food and abandoning himself to grief. A false rumour reaching him that Birbal had escaped with his life the Emperor discarded his mourning, only to assume it a second time on learning that the first report had been correct.

Bir Bal's house is near the north-west corner of Jodh Bai's Palace. Its close proximity to the Imperial stables suggests that he may have been Master of the Horse in addition to being Prime Minister. His residence was separated from the stables by a high wall, and a range of out offices designed on the same plain as the little gabled building still standing to north-west of the house. This small detached edifice bears an inscription on its southern side which describes it as a private hospital.

Not only is Birbal's house the best preserved in Fatehpur Sikri, it rivals that of the Turkish Sultana in the beauty and elaboration of its exterior and interior carving, which is in a harmonious blend of Hindu and Muhammadan styles. It stands upon a massive concrete platform commanding a fine view of the Hathi Pol, Hiran Minar and Karavansarai to north, while, on the west, it overlooked the lake, gay with its flotilla of imperial barges. Built in 1571 by Raja Birbal for his daughter, the house is double storeyed, and contains four apartments on the ground floor, each 16 feet square, and two entrance porches. Steep narrow stairs run up from the north-west and south-east angles to the flat roof, originally enclosed by pierced stone screens through which the ladies of the harem could gaze out on the brilliant and varied panorama around. The other two corners of the roof are occupied by dome crowned apartments remarkable for the thickness of their walls. These are fitted with the cupboards, or recesses so characteristic of Moghul domestic architecture, and display bay windows supported by elaborately sculptured brackets. The ceilings are strikingly beautiful throughout, and afford astonishing proof of the vast amount of skilled manual labour at Akbar's command.

NAGINA MASJID

Near to the north wall of the court containing Birbal's House is the Nagina Masjid, a small mosque reserved for ladies of the zenana. It occupies a stone flagged enclosure, now open on the south side, and measures 24 feet 3 inches by 33 feet 6 inches, the interior divided into two aisles by slender red sandstone pillars. Three mihrabs are sunk in the western wall indicating the direction of Mecca, the Kiblah or spot towards which all followers of Islam must turn when praying. The mimbar, or pulpit, is at right angles to the central mihrab.

In conformity with the Muhammadan custom of encouraging birds about their buildings the upper portion of the south lateral wall is pierced with small arched cavities, or pigeon holes.

A porch, at the northern end, overlooks the road to the Hathi Pol and Hiran Minar, or Deer Tower. To west of the mosque is an almonry, similar to several others in the city, where the destitute were succoured irrespective of creed.

HATHI POL

From the north-west corner of Birbal's House a viaduct originally ran down to the Hathi Pol, and thence onwards through the Karavan Sarai to the Hiran Minar. Now the road passes some ruins close to which are the water works. These consist of a range of buildings dominated by a tank, from which altitude water was distributed to different parts of the palace by means of conduits, portions of which still remain. Turning to the right the road next leads to the Hathi Pol, or Elephant Gate, so called from the immense stone figures of elephants, 13 feet high, that stood on pedestals flanking the outer archway. Aurangzib commanded the statues to be destroyed. Their fragments lie on the ground below the gate to this day, mute, but eloquent witness to that fanatical zeal which broke up a mighty empire.

The great gateway is traversed by a passage 10 feet 9 inches high, and 17 feet 9 inches wide. At either side are guards' chambers sunk in the thickness of the wall above the road level, while staircases run up to the roof and the loop-holed ramparts above the outer face of the portico. Surmounting all is a terrace, 48 feet in length, and an open pavilion. A third staircase connects with the Kabutar Khana, or Pigeon House, and the Sangin Burj.

Rough, uneven boulders pave the road along which Akbar passed mounted in a glittering howdah borne by his favourite elephant.

KABUTAR KHANA

The so-called Pigeon House is of rough rubble masonry plastered on the outside. It was probably used as a powder magazine.

SANGIN BURJ

In close proximity is the Sangin Burj, a grand bastion oined by a gallery to the Hathi Pol on the north-east side.

The Burj, or Tower was commenced by Akbar but abandoned on the advice of Salim Chishti who prophesied that, were Fatehpur Sikri to be fortified on all four sides, the Emperor's greatness would decline.

The bastion consists of an irregular octagon faced with red sandstone, the exterior characterized by deep arched recesses and arched panels of buff-coloured stone. Inside is a central chamber surrounded by six smaller ones and having a verandah on the south. Like the Hathi Pol the Sangin Burj is provided with hooded machicolations through which to pour stones, boiling lead, etc., upon the enemy.

KARAVAN SARAI

From the Elephant Gate, the road leads down through the remains of the Sarai, a vast quadrangle built round with small flat roofed apartments, and a verandah, for the accommodation of travellers and their animals. The main entrance is in the middle of the west wall, and is a double-storeyed portal of imposing aspect. To east is a range of buildings two storeys high. The lower consisted of stables. Amid the ruins may still be seen the stone pegs and rings to which the heel ropes were secured.

HIRAN MINAR

According to tradition this curious tower was built above the remains of Akbar's favourite elephant on the bank of the great artificial lake. It is a reproduction of the still more celebrated minar adorning the courtyard of Hussain's shrine at Kerbela, in Turkish Arabia. The outer walls bristle with stone imitations of elephants tusks, and are plentifully pierced with small star-shaped openings through which light is admitted to the steep spiral staircase within. Octagonal at the base, the Deer Tower becomes round as it ascends, until it finally tapers up to a dome-crowned capital, the open spaces about which were formerly filled in with fret-work screens. A covered passage used to connect the Hiran Minar with the palace. Along this the ladies of the harem passed to climb the fifty-three steps leading to the top of the tower, from which point of vantage they watched aquatic sports on the lake, or looked down upon the Imperial army manœuvring in the plain. From here, too, Akbar is said to have shot deer and other game, and to have witnessed wild beast fights and wrestling bouts.

THE LAKE

Seven miles long, and two miles wide Akbar's great artificial lake formed the western defence of his city. It was fed by the Banganga River and supplied the entire locality. A masterly network of conduits testify to the thoroughness with which the question of water supply was studied when planning the new capital, sprays having been provided to play upon the roofs of some of the palaces during the hot weather.

JAMA MASJID

Retracing his steps the visitor finds himself in the large courtyard of the Jama Masjid, or Great Mosque. Erected in 1571, after the plan of a celebrated shrine at Mecca, it is the largest and grandest building in Fatehpur Sikri. Some authorities pronounce it the finest example of its kind in India. It is not on account of its architectural beauties, however, that it continues to attract so many hundred worshippers, but because of its proximity to the tomb of Salim Chishti, one of the most noted places of Moslem pilgrimage in the country.

The Masjid occupies a site measuring 438 feet from north to south, by 542 feet from east to west. The court is open to the sky. Cloisters surround it on three sides broken by gateways to east and south. The latter is the famous Buland Darwaza towering 176 feet.

The Liwan, or shrine stretches along the western end of the quadrangle, and is crowned by three domes. Inside is a square central chamber between pillared halls, the entire western wall marked by arched mihrabs, richly ornamented, and framed by borders of kashani work, colour decoration showing on the spandrils.

When Akbar, in the heyday of his temporal power, aspired to spiritual dominion over his people, he proceeded to address a congregation in the Jama Masjid at Fatehpur Sikri. The Liwan, the pillared halls and vast quadrangle were thronged with a crowd eager to see and hear the Emperor in his new rôle of High Priest. Faizi had composed some verses, in honour of the occasion for the Emperor to recite :—

The Lord to me the kingdom gave,
He made me wise, and strong, and brave,
He girded me in right and ruth,
Filling my mind with love of truth ;
No praise of man can sum his state
Alla'hu Akbar !—God is great.

A prey to overpowering emotion the Emperor mounted the steps of the Mimbar. Mighty as a monarch, a dauntless leader of armies and a stern, though just judge of those brought before him in the Diwan-i-Am, Akbar was weak as a woman in the presence of his God. In trembling tones he began the inaugural hymn, then the ringing voice broke, and he was obliged to descend, leaving the court chaplain to conclude the service.

DURGAH OF SHAIKH SALIM CHISHTI

Honoured by Moslems as the tomb of a saint, and by others as the most beautiful specimen of early Moghul architecture, the shrine of Pir Salim Chishti stands in the quadrangle of the Great Mosque. Erected in 1581, it is a square building of pure white marble, and measures 47 feet 11 inches each way. On the south side is the portico considered without rival in India as a specimen of white marble carving. The pillars are remarkable. They are Muhammadan reproductions of Dravidian columns belonging to the tenth century Mantapam of a Siva temple in Chidambaram, Madras.

The portico gives access to a marble verandah enclosed by pierced fretwork screens. Light is admitted to the central chamber through delicately perforated screens which fill the three arched window openings. The cenotaph occupies the centre of the marble floor, beneath a beautiful baldachino, or canopy of shisham wood exquisitely inlaid with mother-o'-pearl. The actual grave is in the vault immediately below.

According to tradition the mosaic border, surrounding the casement in the north-east corner, marks the place where Salim was in the habit of praying. The spot is held peculiarly sacred, and it is here that the Imam sits enthroned during the great mela beginning on the 20th Ramazan, the anniversary of the Sheikh's death.

A silver horseshoe used to hang on the door, where it was set by Akbar, but the relic was looted by the Raja of Dholpur.

The shrine is still very much frequented by devotees. Women are not allowed beyond the verandah. All are required to remove their shoes before entering.

It is handed down that shortly before his death, Salim Chishti was warned to provide that his body should be interred at Fatehpur Sikri, and not conveyed thence to Mecca.

TOMB OF ISLAM KHAN

Close by the white marble shrine of Sheikh Salim Chishti is the big red sandstone mausoleum, crowned by a Pathan shaped dome, of his grandson Nawab Islam Khan. This noted descendant of the saint was made Governor of Bengal and married Ladli Begam, sister to those famous men Faizi, the poet, and Abul Fazl, the historian.

Islam's Durgah is surrounded by a wide verandah enclosed by fretted screens, the west side divided up into a series of sepulchral chambers by means of pierced sandstone partitions. The finest is in the south-west corner. This contains two white marble tombs, over which a light burns perpetually.

An elaborate wooden baldachino rises above the Nawab's cenotaph, which stands in the north-west angle of the central chamber, an octagonal apartment chiefly interesting because of the stone door, one of the few still extant. As such it serves to illustrate those once common in the city.

The durgah contains thirty-two other graves, while the female descendants of Islam Khan sleep on its northern side.

Marked features of Moghul architecture are the numerous small kiosks wherewith the roof is decorated.

ZENANA RAUZA

Exactly opposite the Buland Darwaza, to north-west of the mausoleum, is the Zenana Rauza, strictly reserved for ladies of Salim Chishti's family. These are buried in two spacious oblong chambers parallel with the walls of the Masj d.

All the sarcophagi are of stone or marble, with one exception, which is of wood. They are ranged in straight rows the head to the north and the feet pointing south. In all cases the tomb of a woman is distinguished by a carved representation of the takhti or slate, the grave of a man displaying the kalamdan, or pen box.

Generally speaking a Muhammadan grave is seven feet deep. No coffin is used. The body is merely wrapped in a shroud and so laid in the earth. The last sad office is performed by the chief mourner. He inclines the head towards the west. This is done so that, on the Judgment Day, the dead may arise facing Mecca. Another precaution is the placing of planks across the mouth of the grave, a few feet from the bottom, to form a vault in order that, on the first night after internment, the corpse may have room to sit up, when cross-examined by the recording angels Munkir and Nankir, regarding his past life, his faith, and the motives which inspired his acts.

The funeral architecture of the Moghuls is some of the finest in the world. This is the more curious as the Prophet strictly forbade the building of high graves, and prohibited any form of sepulchral monument.

BULAND DARWAZA

Commanding the south side of the vast quadrangle of the mosque is the Buland Darwaza or High Gateway. Aptly named the portal is the largest and loftiest in India, rising 176 feet above the pavement. It was erected by Akbar in 1601, to commemorate his victory over Southern India. On one of the jambs is the celebrated inscription added by Akbar after the conquest of Khandes, converted into Dandesh in honour of his son, Prince Daniel. 'His Majesty the King of Kings, whose Court is Paradise, Shadow of God, Jalal-ud-Din Muhammed, the Emperor. He conquered the Deccan and Dandes, which was formerly Khandes, in the Ilaki year 46, corresponding to the Hijra year 1010.'

The inscription concludes:—'Said Jesus—on whom be peace—The world is a bridge, pass over it but build no house. He who hopes for an hour hopes for an eternity. The world is but an hour. Spend it in devotion. The rest is unseen.'

Four years later Akbar died.

Innumerable domes, both large and small, surmount the triumphal gateway after the fashion characteristic of Moghul architecture.

THE GREAT WELL

Not quite half-way down the steep steps leading from Akbar's triumphal arch, a narrow passage on the right, turns sharply back to a huge baoli, or well thirty-two feet in diameter.

BADSHAH DARWAZA

On the eastern side of the mosque quadrangle the gateway is known as the Badshah Darwaza, or Emperor's Gate, from the fact that the Emperor passed through it daily on his way to prayers in the Jama Masjid.

ABUL FAZL'S HOUSE

In the rear of the Zenana Rauza, and abutting on to the north-west wall of the Jama Masjid, are the neighbouring houses of the celebrated brothers Faizi and Abul Fazl. The latter was Akbar's dearly loved friend and favourite wazir, as well as the most famous historian of the age. Faizi was Poet Laureate. Both were converts to Akbar's new religion, the Tauhid-i-Ilahi, or Divine Monotheism.

Abul Fazl was born in 1551, and assumed the *nom de plume* of Allami. He was introduced to Akbar in the ninteenth year of that Emperor's reign. The historian was then just twenty-four and the Emperor thirty-three. Abul Fazl is for ever noted as the author of the *Ain-i-Akbari*, the *Akbarnama* and the *Maktubat-i-Allama*. Apart from the immense historical value of these works, their literary style proves Abul Fazl to have been the most elegant, as well as the most learned writer of the period.

Unfortunately he excited the jealousy of the heir apparent, Prince Salim, afterwards Jahangir Shah. This prince caused him to be murdered on Friday, August 13, 1602. At the moment of his death Abul Fazl was returning to Agra flushed with victory, having led a successful expedition against the celebrated fort of Asigarh. On hearing of the assassination, and learning the instigator of it, Akbar was overwhelmed with grief. For two days he neither eat nor slept.

The houses of the brothers stand within a walled enclosure, but a few paces separating the one from the other. Abul Fazl lived in the first. His dwelling is characterized by a long pillared verandah, which still bears traces of beautiful and elaborate carving. On the ground floor two small rooms flank a large central chamber measuring thirty-nine feet by seventeen feet. A row of domed baths lie to south of the building which Abul Fazl occupied with his wife, a sister of the Raja of Khandesh.

FAIZI'S HOUSE

The house of the Poet Laureate also displays a verandah in front, and consisted of three ground floor apartments, the large chamber, on the upper storey, being reserved for the zenana. All the ceilings were painted in geometrical designs in white on a royal blue ground. The flat roof was converted into a screened promenade for the ladies of the family by means of high walls of pierced sandstone.

In 1592 Faizi was sent as ambassador to the Deccan but returned to Agra before his death, which occurred on October 5, 1595. It is told how, shortly before he passed away, he received a visit from Akbar. Sorely distressed at his friend's condition the Emperor raised the dying head urging, 'Shekhji, here is a doctor! Will you not speak to me.' Receiving no reply, the King of Kings flung his turban on the ground and wept aloud.

Both the house of Faizi and of Abul Fazl are now used as

a Zilla School. In Faizi's, English is taught, that of Abul Fazl being devoted to instruction in the vernacular.

STONE CUTTERS' MOSQUE

This humble sanctuary lies to the west of the Jama Masjid. Long before the advent of Akbar upon the scenes it was built for Sheikh Salim Chishti, by the devout stone cutters. Tradition avers that somewhere, within its precincts, is the jealously hidden cave once occupied by the saint.

RANG MAHAL

Near by is the ruined house wherein Jahangir was born. It was originally named the Rang Mahal. The chamber pointed out as an Emperor's birth-place is on the ground floor. It is a small room measuring 9 feet 6 inches by 8 feet 4 inches, the ceiling supported by a plain pillar in the middle. The house was the residence of Salim Chishti and contains another apartment of interest as having been the scene of the Sheikh's most rigorous penances. The wagon vaulted roof of this apartment is crossed by two stone beams from which Salim Chishti is said to have hung head downwards for hours at a time while telling his beads. The encircling walls are three feet thick, but even so time has not spared the dwelling of a saint, and the birth-place of an Emperor.

HISTORY

Of Agra's early history little or nothing is known. Even tradition is silent on the subject. Whence it first sprang into being, and from what source it drew its name are alike shrouded in impenetrable mystery. That it existed at all, prior to Mussulman days, might well be doubted but for a statement by Salman, a Persian poet who died in 1131. He tells how the fortress of Agra, was wrested from Jaipal by Mahmud, after a desperate assault. The light thus thrown is but a temporary flash of illumination. Immediately afterwards the history of the city plunges back into its former obscurity. From this it emerges upon the advent of Sikandar Lodi. In 1492 Agra is heard of as besieged by this monarch. Apparently the place relied for its defence upon the fortress of Badalgarh, said to have been erected by Badal Singh about 1475. Tradition also goes on to assert that the present great sandstone castle, built by Akbar, stands on or near the earlier structure. Some authorities dispute this, declaring the fortress and city of that day to have occupied the opposite bank of the Jumna.

Lodi Dynasty.—After he had taken Agra, Sikandar Lodi appointed a governor over the place, while he pursued his victorious campaign in other directions. Before long he found it necessary to establish permanent head-quarters, and selected the town on the banks of the Jumna as best for his purpose. Here he set about erecting a city which he made his capital.

Several authorities incline to the belief that the village of Sikandarah, five miles outside Agra, was the site chosen by Sikandar Lodi. In support of this they point to the still surviving baradari built by him, at that place, in 1495.

Nothing very conclusive can be said for or against this theory. All that is really settled is that Agra became the definite seat of Government from then on. In 1505 a severe earthquake destroyed many of the newly-erected buildings, but of their number and just where they were situated, no record exists. Sikandar died at Agra in 1517 and was succeeded by Ibrahim Lodi.

Baber.—The battle of Paniput in 1526 resulted in Ibraham Lodi's defeat and death. The victorious Baber immediately sent Humayun forward to Agra to seize the treasure and take possession. The jewels which then fell into the Moghul's hands are said to have included the famous diamond known at the Koh-i-nur.

'Tis an ill wind that blows nobody good.' Agra benefited greatly by her change of conquerors. Baber made roads, planted gardens, constructed water courses and established the familiar Persian wheel, thanks to which the desert is made to blossom like the rose. In 1530 he died at Agra, whence his body was conveyed to Kabul for burial.

Humayun.—Three days after his father's death Humayun was crowned in the palace at Agra. The first ten years of his reign were spent more in this city than at Delhi, but the majority of his time was passed at the head of his forces in the field. In 1530 he was severely defeated by Sher Shah, and driven to take refuge in flight. While retreating through the desert of Sind, on his way to Persia, his famous son Akbar was born in the small fort of Umarkot in 1542.

Sher Shah.—After defeating Baber, Sher Shah established himself at Agra. He built a palace on the site now occupied by Akbar's Fort, and maintained his supremacy until his death, from an accident, in 1545.

Quarrels among his successors led to troublous days for Agra. Badaumi tells of a terrible famine that visited the place, and an explosion which shattered the Fort immediately prior to Ibrahim Singh's occupation of that city.

Akbar.—Humayun died at Delhi in 1556, and was at once succeeded by his son Akbar, a lad of fourteen. The reign of this great Moghul lasted nearly fifty years. He was a contemporary of Queen Elizabeth of England (Akbar 1556—1605, Elizabeth, 1558—1603). In 1558 he proceeded to Agra, making his capital in that city instead of at Delhi. He commenced to build the palace in 1565, the chief constructor being Qasim Khan, the commander of the boats. On his return from capturing the celebrated stronghold of Rantambhor, he paid a visit to Sheikh Salim Chishti and shortly afterwards began to erect the city of Fatehpur Sikri. It was his intention to make it his capital, and he spent much of his time there. Towards the end of his reign political considerations led him to return to Agra, where he died in 1605, and was buried at Sikandarah.

His reign was famous, less for the magnitude and importance of his conquests than for the reforms he inaugurated. He placed all his subjects on an equal political footing, gave high posts to Hindus and did his best to abolish the burning of widows. In this last effort he was not successful, but he took steps to make sure that the sacrifice was a voluntary one.

Jahangir.—Jahangir succeeded his father and was crowned in the palace at Agra. Much of his reign was disturbed by the rebellion of his sons. In 1622 Prince Khurram, afterwards Shah Jahan, seized Fatehpur Sikri and marched on Agra, where he plundered the city and proceeded to Muttra. It was during Jahangir's reign that James I sent a letter to the Moghul Emperor by the hand of Captain William Hawkins. The Envoy from the British monarch was well received and remained three years at Agra. Five years later Thomas Kerridge was sent to Agra, where he established a cloth factory. This was abandoned in 1617, owing to poor trade. In 1613 Sir Robert and Lady Shirley visited Agra on their way to Persia, and several other British travellers found their way to the capital about the same time. Finally Jahangir died at Lahore in 1628 and was buried in that city.

Shah Jahan.—In February, 1628, Prince Khurram was proclaimed Emperor at Agra, assuming the title of Shah Jahan. He removed his capital to Delhi but much of his time was spent at Agra where he was ultimately imprisoned in the palace by his rebellious son, Aurangzib. There he died in December, 1666, and was buried in the Taj Mahal with his favourite wife.

It is to the tombs of the Moghuls that we owe some of the most splendid examples of their architectural style. Their passion for this form of building was quite as remarkable as that which distinguished the ancient Egyptians. They did not entrust the work of providing a suitable mausoleum for their remains to their successors. In his life-time an emperor or wealthy noble generally laid out a beautiful garden. He enclosed it with high walls and magnificent gateways, made water channels and fountains, and erected a platform from which radiated four-paved walls. In the midst he built a square, or octagonal edifice crowned by one or more domes, and very often adorned it with tall minarets. While he lived this was known as a Bara Dari, or festal hall, and was used as such by him and his friends. Directly he died, all this was changed. His body was solemnly conveyed to the lower vault of the building converted by his death into a mausoleum, which was henceforth handed over to the charge of Priests.

Aurangzib.—After the death of his father, Aurangzib does not appear to have resided at Agra. Delhi was his capital until 1682, when he removed the seat of Government to

Ahmadabad and thence to Burhanpur. His reign, like those of Jahan, Jahangir and Akbar was made wretched by rebellious sons.

His Successors.—Aurangzib died in 1707. He left a will dividing his empire between his three sons. Muazzam was allotted Delhi, with the northern and eastern provinces. Bijapur and Golconda were assigned to Kam Baksh, while Azam was given Agra with the rest of India as his kingdom. Civil war followed between the brothers. Agra suffered considerably, and was sacked by the Saiyids, who took advantage of the general confusion to seize the vast accumulation of treasure, loot the tombs of Shah Jahan and Mumtaz-i-Mahal, and carry off the famous pall of pearls laid over the cenotaph of the Empress on Friday nights and on the anniversary of her wedding.

British Occupation.—In turn Jats and Marathas succeeded in becoming masters of Agra. The city was constantly changing hands until captured by Lord Lake in 1803. A hundred and sixty-four cannon were found inside the fort. These included the great gun of Akbar, a brass twenty-three inch piece of 7·4 calibre and forty-three tons weight, carrying a ball of 1,500 lbs. This ancient cannon was supposed to be composed of all the precious metals, and native money changers are said to have offered a lakh of rupees for it. Lord Lake, however, decided to send it to England. It was placed on a raft and floated down the Jumna, but suddenly capsized.

Few traces of the troubled past are observable in the Agra of to-day. It has developed into an important educational centre, but it is not its modern buildings, its schools, houses and colleges, which attract visitors to Agra. It is the Taj Mahal they come to see and, having seen, are almost sorry that they came. The wondrous white shrine casts a lasting spell over those who pass its magic portals. They are evermore haunted by the perfume of dying flowers scattered on a jewelled tomb, by the ghostly play of shadows behind marble screens, and by echoes from a lofty dome, sweet and melancholy echoes from whose whisper there is no escape. *Non ti scorda di me.* ('Forget-me-not.')

JAIPUR HOTEL

JAIPUR, RAJPUTANA

UNDER THE PATRONAGE OF HIS HIGHNESS THE MAHARAJA

An entirely new palatial edifice, built by His Highness the Maharaja, double storied, with marble plaster flooring and open verandahs overlooking beautiful spacious grounds, and a delightful view of the hills and Fort, situated near all places of interest and the Residency. The first class, largest and Ideal New Hotel in Jaipur, furnished with new furniture and lighted with incandescent gas.

ACCOMMODATION

Excellent, well ventilated, single and double bedrooms, each with fireplace and bath and large dressing rooms. Sanitary arrangements on the most modern principle. Thorough cleanliness is kept. Particular attention is paid to the Cuisine. Carriage, Elephants, Automobiles and all kinds of conveyances ready at call.

No tourist should miss seeing this wonderful Rajput city in India

COOK'S COUPONS ACCEPTED

NOWROJI JAMSETJI,
Managing Proprietor.

'BOMBAY: The Gate of India'

Some LONDON Press Opinions:

The Times: 'Major NEWELL has written a good many guides which have been published in India. The present one is the first he has published in London: and Anglo-Indians or travellers visiting India will find it a compact and useful publication with all kinds of information succinctly given and its three days' itinerary described.'

The Globe: 'Major H. A. NEWELL, of the Indian Army, who is now at the front, is the author of a number of most useful guides to various towns and districts in our great Dependency . . . . Contains a capital map as well as much information of interest and value about the city and its environs. . . Few cities are better worth knowing.'

The Standard: ' . . . as is the case in his other publications the author displays a happy way of holding the interest of his reader, so that in addition to being an invaluable help to the visitor, the volume possesses the merit of being a literary effort of considerable excellence. A capital map is included . .

Truth: 'Major H. A. NEWELL, Indian Army, completed another of his attractive little guide books to Indian cities before he went on active service with the Expeditionary Force. "Bombay: The Gate of India" is the subject, and in his usual pleasant style he sketches the city's history and describes the places of interest that should be visited by the traveller with two or three days to spare there.'

Outlook: 'With a thorough knowledge of the city Major Newell (who is now on active service in France) gives a short history of Bombay, and a description of the many places of interest, together with a map,' etc., etc.

The Pioneer says:

'Major NEWELL's guide books are well known for their accuracy and for the wealth of information they contain. . . .'

The Chattanooga News, U.S A., says:

'Major NEWELL, the author of this delightful guide book, is now on active service in France. When peace comes he will have to write up his view of the war. He can do it, for his wide culture will then find full play, and he is a student of history. In this little book is all the necessary advice needed by the tourist as to what, or when to see: hotels, routes, values of money, etc., are given. . . .'

Sunday Times: 'Major H. A. NEWELL, of the Indian Army, has compiled a number of guide books of the principal cities in India. They contain a wealth of valuable information with regard to social customs, hotels, routes, value of moneys, etc. Tourists will find these books not only useful, but will be fascinated by their literary excellence and the extent of historical knowledge which the writer shows.'

'LUCKNOW: The Capital of Oudh'

Asiatic Quarterly Review: 'As a compiler of guide books dealing with some of the great cities of India, Major Newell is now widely known in the Dependency. The brochure to Lucknow will add greatly to his renown as a reliable cicerone . . . . Major Newell's description of the places of interest in the city is interesting and accurate. The short chapter dealing with the history of Lucknow makes the book invaluable as a guide book.'

Mrs. Sarojini Naidu, the celebrated poetess, writes:—

'Thank you so much for kindly sending me a copy of your interesting little guide to Lucknow. I am sure it will receive the cordial reception it deserves from the hosts of visitors who make a pilgrimage every year to The Garden City.'

Evening News, Chattanooga, Tenn. U.S.A.: 'The entire series of the author's guide books is invested with the charm of high culture; they are books to read as well as use in travel, poetical as well as practical.'

PRINTED AT THE S.P.C.K. PRESS, VEPERY, MADRAS—1919 C11302.